- Solving Management's Puzzle -

The Art of Managing People

David Anthony Korponai

Note for Librarians: A cataloguing record for this book is available from Library
and Archives Canada at www.collectionscanada.ca/amicus/index-e.html

Printed in Victoria, BC, Canada.

ISBN: 978-1-4251-8500-8

Library of Congress Control Number:

*We at Trafford believe that it is the responsibility of us all, as both individuals and corporations,
to make choices that are environmentally and socially sound. You, in turn, are supporting this
responsible conduct each time you purchase a Trafford book, or make use of our publishing services.
To find out how you are helping, please visit www.trafford.com/responsiblepublishing.html*

*Our mission is to efficiently provide the world's finest, most comprehensive book publishing
service, enabling every author to experience success. To find out how to publish your book, your
way, and have it available worldwide, visit us online at www.trafford.com*

Trafford rev.

 **www.trafford.com**

North America & international
toll-free: 1 888 232 4444 (USA & Canada)
phone: 250 383 6864 ♦ fax: 250 383 6804 ♦ email: info@trafford.com

Contents

STATEMENT

AS A PERSONAL Services Contract employee of a United States Government agency, I would like to make one point perfectly clear. I am reasonably assured that there is nothing in this printed text that is of an official concern. Therefore, this text is not subject to any clearance procedures and is in compliance with 3 FAM 4170.

All opinions and views expressed herein are those of the Author and not necessarily those of the United States Agency for International Development or any other U.S. Government agency.

OPENING

IN MAY 1993 I attended the graduation of my daughter, Karen. She graduated from the University of Colorado, Boulder with majors in International Affairs-Latin America and Spanish Business.

Karen was interested in going beyond the classroom. She wanted to further educate herself about working and managing in a real work environment. She took it upon herself to intern with the State of Colorado International Trade Office during her senior year. She developed a student-mentor relationship with one of her professors and read books outside of the normally assigned reading materials.

[A tangent note related to a "real work environment." In the context of this book it means an environment that is a balance between people and devices. Or an environment skewed to the people side. As we get more and more hi-tech it seems to me like we are getting closer and closer to creating a "faceless" work environment.]

One of the books that Karen read was Covey's, *The 7 Habits of Highly Effective People* that she nonchalantly tossed on my lap one day to read. My first reaction was one of, "Only seven habits?" I have more than seven, albeit, all of them may not be good habits. They may not have made me a highly effective person, but nonetheless I have more than seven.

[I may have been on to something here as I see that Covey has a new book out; *The 8th Habit – From Effectiveness to Greatness*. Will the 9th habit take you from "Greatness to God?"]

While all of my habits may not have led me to become a highly effective person, I believe that I had proven myself to be a damn good and highly effective manager over the years. To begin with, my work habits, and recognition and awareness of what went on in the work environment and around me led to my more effective management of the human, financial and the other resources that I managed.

Having rapidly skimmed over the Table of Contents of *The 7 Habits* ... I began to think about - *what would make managers, better and more effective regardless of their management style, individual personality or habits.*

The common denominators to me were: *(1)Identification;* what are the pieces, elements, components, factors or ingredients needed to manage more effectively? *(2) Continued Awareness;* of what has been identified and developing an understanding as to why they are important and,*(3) Application;* how and when can they be used in our everyday work environment.

The line of reasoning then is that once these elements are identified and we develop a continued awareness of them their application will help us become better managers. They will assist in developing or modifying the way that we manage or supervise. This will help us to hone our management skills and help us to focus on the art of managing and solving our everyday management puzzles. *The result will be more effective management or supervision of all of our resources.*

What have been identified here are those elements in the *"real"* work environment that a manager should be aware of that will lead to more effective management. Once we settle on these we can then begin the learning process that leads to even more effective management. I said settle on, not agree on as we may have some differences of opinion as to what elements should, or should not be included in this discussion.

This is not textbook management where hypothetical situations and textbook solutions are presented. We'll get into real life, grass-roots, down and dirty examples and situations.

Most of these will be based on personal experiences and knowledge gained at various levels of participation on the gridiron, on the battlefield and in the board room. In their own way, the boardroom and the real work environment are battlefields. Regarding the boardroom, *more* effective managers will reduce wars to skirmishes leading to a more harmonious work environment – harmonious; not perfect or pure!

CHAPTER I

---◆◆---

INTRODUCTION

THIS BOOK PROVIDES you with an unsophisticated look at the art of managing people through the eyes of a "grass-roots" manager. It was written in an informal tone and plain language.

The theme of this book was developed around several ideas. One of which is that self-evaluation will lead to self-confidence and self-satisfaction that will lead to greater successes. The art of managing other people begins with knowing and understanding yourself.

I strongly believe that everyone, from those on the lowest rung on the corporate ladder or organizational   chart to the highest ranking corporate executive needs a little jump start every once in a while. This book does just that. It is a reminder just as much as it is a learning tool. This book will make you think and will help you to better exercise your free will in the work environment. For some, it will be a real eye opener.

Furthermore, if you are not an effective manager already, this book will provide the bridge that will help you go from an average manager to a more effective manager. If you are already an effective manager, this book will help you to become even more effective in what you do. Get the picture? There is something in here for everyone.

Some of what has been written here may sound unconventional or controversial to some of you. You may not agree with everything that is between these covers. That's fine with me. As we shall discover, more effective managers welcome differences of opinion and the subsequent challenges that come along with these differences.

To manage is "to direct, supervise, or carry on business or other affairs." To be effective is to produce a desired impression or response. *An effective manager then is someone who can produce desired impressions or responses while he directs, supervises, or carries on business or other affairs.*

The desired impression or response can relate to how he conducts his own business or personal affairs. It can also relate to how others respond to his direction or supervision.

4

This book focuses on the latter; management or supervision of others in the ever changing, fast-paced, multi-dimensional work environment. For the purpose of this book, the words "manager" and "supervisor"; "managing" and "supervising"; and, "management" and "supervision" are synonymous.

More effective management is not that difficult. Does it also involve the most uncommon sense of all - common sense? Does it involve a little bit of luck? If you answered, "yes" to both questions you are absolutely correct.

More effective management also involves being and staying aware of, and focusing of those elements that can lead to improving the way that you manage. Once you are aware of these elements, you can begin your self-evaluation of how you manage. You can identify those elements that you are weakest in and work on developing those skills and techniques that will help you overcome or strengthen these weaknesses. This will help you to become a wiser, better and more effective manager.

This book is designed to do just that; make you aware of, and to help you focus on those elements or areas that, once applied, will help you to manage more effectively. The examples of real-life experiences mentioned in the discussion of some of the awareness elements will provide you with a clearer picture of what is being discussed. Some may appear to be individual oriented, but all flow into and can be incorporated into the work environment.

This is *not* a "how-to-do" or a "how-to-manage" book. View it as self-help. Once again, although focusing on the work environment, these same elements can be put to use in your personal, every day activities. The knowledge that you gain from reading this will not only help you in your life as a manager, but in your personal life too.

Management is like putting together a puzzle. You do not always put the pieces together in the same sequence. Visualize more effective management as being that puzzle.

The pieces are the awareness elements that you need to put together the puzzle. Different situations will dictate the sequence in which you will put the pieces together. They are all important. The first piece starts the process, the middle pieces form the big picture and begin to bring clarity to the picture and the last piece completes the picture. The bottom line is to complete the puzzle - to manage more effectively - to become a better manager than you already are.

As you will see, some of these elements, while distinct in themselves may have some over-lapping, cross-cutting implications. This natural connectivity leads to these pieces fitting nicely together to solve our management puzzle.

You may also find that some of these elements are more dominant than others when considered in your overall solution. This goes hand in glove with a later discussion: While everything is important, depending on the time and on the situation some things (elements) may be more important than others.

After reading this book you will come away with the ability to focus, or refocus on those elements that will help you to manage more effectively. You may have some of these in your bag of management tools already.

Believe me, these pieces will fall into place easier than you might expect. Throughout this book you will see how they come together and complement one another to complete the picture.

One other point to remember; you do not have to be a member of MENSA or have an IQ of 150 or be a Harvard graduate to be a more effective manager. Your success as a manager is more related to your awareness of what it takes to become a better and more effective manager and your awareness of what is going on around you, than it is to how intelligent you are.

Read on, relax and enjoy yourself on your way to becoming a shrewder, better, more intelligent, wiser and more effective manager, and person in the real work environment. It's not that difficult.

CHAPTER II

ABOUT THE AUTHOR, BY THE AUTHOR

BEFORE BEGINNING THIS book, let me answer the one question that must be nagging some of you, "Who the hell is David Anthony Korponai?" This is a fair question that deserves an honest answer.

In a nutshell - After graduating from high school in Stratford, Connecticut I attended the University of Connecticut in Storrs. In addition to pursuing an education, I joined a fraternity (Alpha Sigma Phi), became involved in various campus activities and captained the UConn football team in my senior year.

My academic credentials upon graduation in June 1964 consisted of one year of general engineering courses (civil engineering was calling me my freshman year), one-half semester of general business courses; and two and one-half years of education courses which led to a Bachelor of Science degree in Physical Education.

During my junior year I was inducted into the ARCHONS, a service group of campus leaders. I also spent countless hours doing community service in the recreational program offered to residents in the town of Manchester, Connecticut. Through all of this, I did my utmost to make a positive contribution towards UConn's reputation as one of the top ten partying colleges and universities in America.

As an ROTC Distinguished Military Graduate, I accepted a regular Army appointment and was commissioned a 2nd Lieutenant in the United States Army. This was also in June 1964.

My fourteen year military career began when I was assigned as the Executive Officer for the Cooks School at Fort Dix, New Jersey - two days after graduating from UConn. This was followed, in rapid succession by my attendance of the Infantry Officer's Basic Course, Ranger School and Airborne School, all at Fort Benning, Georgia.

My overseas assignments, in order were Germany, Vietnam, Bolivia and again Vietnam.

My stateside assignments, in order, were Fort Dix, New Jersey; Fort Benning, Georgia; Fort Benjamin Harrison, Indiana, where, as a junior Captain I attended the Adjutants Generals Corp Advance Course; Fort Monmouth, New Jersey; and finally the Armed Forces Entrance and Examining Station in beautiful downtown Newark, New Jersey, where I was honorably discharged at the rank of captain in November 1978.

I spent almost six years in overseas assignments. I was awarded numerous letters of commendation and appreciation and two Bronze Star Medals for Meritorious Achievement, two Army Commendation Medals for Meritorious Achievement and two Joint Service Commendation Medals for Meritorious Achievement.

My most challenging and rewarding assignment was Chief of a Military Personnel Branch at Fort Monmouth, New Jersey, where, as a junior captain I filled this Major's position for more than two years. This branch was staffed by 105 men and women, both military and civilian.

My career in the private sector began in earnest in January 1979 when I returned to Bolivia with one wife, three young children, one dog and one cat - and, no job! Having sold our house in New Jersey and pooling resources, I gave myself six months to find gainful employment in the heart of South America.

I began this new adventure by accepting employment with the S.J. Groves & Sons Company. Groves & Sons was a large, Minneapolis based, American heavy construction company operating in Bolivia. They were building a forty-eight kilometer road from La Paz to Cotapata and a series of five bridges. I rose fairly quickly from a local hire with no fringe benefits, to the Administrative/Financial Manager, with full benefits for this 68 million U.S. dollar project.

Upon termination of the Groves & Sons project in April 1984, I was between jobs. I spent the next two years or so making ends meet by doing a variety of jobs which included consulting to several Bolivian companies, exchanging money and, on one occasion transporting dead, but plucked chickens from Cochabamba, to La Paz.

I also had a short stint of three months with the Narcotic's Assistance Unit of the American Embassy in La Paz, Bolivia. My title was the Coca Reduction Field Advisor and I spent most of my time in the largest coca growing area of Bolivia - the Chapare Valley in Cochabamba. Believe it or not, I recommended that this position be deleted! The reason - The program was so poorly designed that it was embarrassing to admit being a part of it as a U.S. Government employee; more about this later.

In August, 1986 I was hired by the R.A. Hanson Company (RaHCO) and served as their South American representative. This extremely innovative and well managed American company was based in Spokane, Washington. RaHCO was involved in mining and selling specialty equipment in the mining and heavy construction/earth moving sectors.

I represented RaHCO for almost two and one-half years. I traveled to Chile, Ecuador and Brazil evaluating business opportunities in the mining sector.

When the owner, despite my protest decided to terminate his activities in South America rather than transfer the operation from La Paz, Bolivia, to Santiago, Chile where there was more potential and a more lucrative market I was again, between jobs. During this time I was asked to join, and accepted membership into the only English-speaking Masonic lodge in Bolivia, Anglo-Bolivian Lodge No. 7.

Having gone past my self imposed time frame to find employment in Bolivia, I returned to the United States in late 1989 and found employment in Connecticut with a small, but highly successful industrial maintenance company, The Kaffen Company, Inc. I was employed as a working foreman. The company was mostly involved in concrete and tile floor repair and restoration and the painting of warehouses and storage tanks.

Believe me when I say that constructing scaffolding that reaches forty foot in height, operating a forty-foot extension boom or a jack hammer, scraping and grinding off old floor coatings on one's hands and knees, and smelling the pungent aroma of resins and acrylics is a far cry from the office environment. However, on the positive side it was a welcome relief from the doldrums of being unemployed.

While with the Kaffen Company I also learned something more about the management of human resources. I worked along side the company's owner (a high school and college friend) and his three full-time employees. In addition, temporary hire employees, mostly wrenched from the inner-city work program were used.

The composition of our work group at any one time consisted of college graduates, high school graduates and drop outs and recovering or recovered alcoholics and substance abuse users. Interacting with and supervising this diverse work force at four o'clock in the morning was not only a test of one's managerial skills, but a test of one's character as well.

I also learned more about myself.

In January 1991, I applied for and was selected for the position of the General Services Officer for the United States Agency for International Development (USAID) mission in La Paz, Bolivia. My venture into the public sector began. I was fortunate enough to begin this career by working *with,* not *for* an executive officer who had vision, set high standards for himself and those who worked with him and was strongly committed to making the work environment a better place to work in. Improving quality of life in the workplace for employees was one of his major goals.

I managed a fifty-five person General Services Office. This position focused on customer service and providing general logistical support to the Mission and its almost one hundred and fifty employees. The areas I managed included: customs; management of almost 4.5 million U.S. dollars worth of non-expendable and expendable property and vehicles; real property management (leasing and maintenance of thirty-two houses and apartments); procurement of materials and services; and, vehicle support/motor pool activities.

Moving up, I then accepted the position of Deputy Executive Officer, in La Paz where I oversaw the General Services Office, the Personnel Office and the Missions' Communications and Records Office while acting as the alter ego to the Executive Officer during his absences. All of this was coupled with normal "deputy" type duties that included taking care of the daily business activities in the Executive Office, attending meetings that no one else wanted to attend and answering the telephone when the secretary was in the water closet.

Staying in the USAID family, I followed La Paz with over five years of service with USAID/Cairo Egypt as the Supervisory General Services Officer. This was, and still may be the largest USAID Mission in the world. When I arrived this Mission had over 100 apartments in its' housing portfolio and over 350 American and Egyptian employees.

This was followed by almost eighteen months as the Executive Officer for USAID Almaty, Kazakhstan, a regional Mission supporting five countries; Kazakhstan, Uzbekistan, Tajikistan, Turkmenistan and Kyrgyzstan.

After a break in employment of about four months, I accepted the position as the Deputy Executive Officer for USAID Kiev, Ukraine. This large Mission was also regional and supported three countries; Ukraine, Moldova and Belarus. I was again lucky enough to work *with*, not *for* a very creative and vibrant executive officer who had "unlimited potential" written all over her. Her move from the Executive Officer ranks to upper management (Deputy Mission Director) positions proved me to be right on target.

After almost five years in Kiev I was selected for the Executive Officer position for the USAID Mission in Podgorica, Serbia/Montenegro. In addition to handling USAID business I also supervised the unit responsible for providing most of the administrative and logistical support to other agencies including the Department of State, the Department of Commerce and the Department of Defense.

When Montenegro gained her independence in May, 2006 I became involved in the unique and oftentimes overly bureaucratic exercise of transforming an American Consulate into a full-fledged American Embassy. And, the additional duty of a Department of State (DOS) Management Officer was thrust upon me. Being exposed to, and learning the DOS "corporate culture" was challenging, exciting, rewarding and frustrating - all wrapped into one.

But to bring this to closure, I will note that damn near all of my assignments and positions that I held in the military and private and public sectors, in themselves and collectively turned out to be learning experiences, par excellence. There were many more positives than there were negatives.

I also discovered that there were a lot of people oriented, caring and professional executives and managers out there. Unfortunately, they did not vastly outnumber the one's who were one-dimensional thinkers and often-times prone to micromanaging and put personal gains and career ahead of their office relationships and responsibilities (Keep note of this). Closing with a positive, I found that most people in either group had the talent, if not the motivation to become even more effective managers than they already were.

CHAPTER III

REALITY CHECKLIST

OK! CHAPTER II is now passé, let's roll up our sleeves and get down to business. What are the reality checks that you should be aware of, focus on and apply to become an even more effective manager than you are now? While all of these can also be applied to the management of your personal affairs, once more what follows in this chapter is directed towards managing and supervising in the multi-dimensional, real work environment. Keep in mind that you will see that there is some connectivity in how you conduct your personal affairs and yourself in the work environment.

There is one last point of order. At the risk of sounding "sexist", as the English language has no neutral singular pronoun, I have used the words "he" and "she" in the text. It's easy. When you see a "he", it could refer to a "he" or a "she"; when you see a "she", it could refer to a "she" or a "he." And, a "him" could refer to a "him" or a "her," and a "her" could refer to a "her" or a "him."

That's enough of Dr. Seuss' prosaic style. I hope that the use of these words is not only grammatically correct, but gender acceptable as well. I'll give credit where credit is due. I owe this to my son David, who took the time to read my first draft manuscript and point out to me its unintentionally sexist tone.

It is now time to look through the Window of Reality and into the real, ever changing, multi-dimensional and fast-paced work environment.

YOUR MOST PRECIOUS RESOURCE; PEOPLE:

A More Effective Manager recognizes that an organization's most precious resource is people.

Someone could probably write an entire book on this subject; or maybe someone already has. The "people theme" will keep appearing throughout this book. You will see it repeated in various different yet complementing ways. It will be further developed in other awareness elements that talk about performance evaluation and training.

I once overheard a Total Quality Management (TQM) guru mention and emphasize that everyone is your customer. This is absolutely correct. This also includes the people that you supervise. I believe that for a more effective manager to fully understand and appreciate this concept, he must become a *people oriented person.*

A more effective manager knows the importance of not only hiring good people but he also understands the importance of *retaining* good people. If you are not in the Personnel Office or directly involved in the selection process of new employees for your unit, do whatever it takes to get involved. Your input is invaluable in the selection process.

Retention of good people allows for continuity in the work environment and in the long run is more cost effective to the company. While the impact may be different in any given company, let me illustrate this by the following example.

A U.S. Government (USG) organization that I am familiar with hired, and trained someone to fill a one-of-a-kind position. The employee was given a two year contract at an overseas location. The cost of all training and training related expenses during this two year period was in the neighborhood of $11,000. The cost of this recruiting action, to include a physical examination, security investigation and job interview was approximately $6,000. The whole recruiting and hiring process, including a background security check took between six and nine months.

In short, the USG had an investment in this person of at least $17,000.

When it came time for a contract renewal, the employee asked for the "fringe benefit" of a housing allowance. The cost of this would have been in the vicinity of $13,000 over two years.

The employee, however, was not only denied this "bennie" but was told that she could not even negotiate the issue. Why? - Because it "just wasn't done." Management had been led to believe that providing this benefit would mean that other employees in her category would automatically be entitled to this benefit.

Not so. This was not an entitlement, but a fringe benefit that could have been negotiated for prior to the contract renewal. A management tool to retain a good employee?

So, what happened? The six to nine month recruitment and hiring cycle had to start all over again. And, the new employee had to go through similar training.

Separation costs, estimated at a tad over $5,000 were also incurred for the departing employee. From a cost standpoint, the "net" to the employer (USG) was a loss of over twenty thousand dollars.

Let me lay emphasis on one point again: an employer makes an investment in each of their employees. You as a more effective manager must realize this. In addition to the costs involved, look at the time that it may take for a new employee to develop rapport with you and with other co-workers. The time to get to "know the ropes" in the company, and the time it might take him personally to adjust to the new work environment. Most of this means less productivity.

In the first year alone that S.J. Groves & Sons was in Bolivia, nearly twenty American employees failed to complete the first year of their contract. All of these employees were hired in the United States and sent to Bolivia, some with their families. Imagine the transportation costs involved.

In the Grove's case most of the problem could be traced to the recruitment process and not management's or line supervisors (in Bolivia) lack of interest in retaining these people at the project site. During the recruitment interview, a prospective employee was shown a lovely picture of a small resort village. It was about a five-hour drive from where they would actually be working and living. Very little was mentioned of the working conditions at 16,000 feet above sea level in the Andes Mountains.

Recruitment begins with transparency.

Let's switch for a moment from the private to the public sector and its foreign service employees working temporarily in overseas places like: La Paz, Bolivia; Cairo, Egypt; Almaty, Kazakhstan; Kiev, Ukraine; or, Podgorica, Montenegro. These are not extensions of an employee's home town or Washington, D.C. New employees have to understand that honoring their commitment to carrying out USG policy in a foreign environment may mean that there will be no Coco Puffs for breakfast or Gummy Bears to munch on. Or worst yet to some, no multi-channel satellite TV or cable will undoubtedly mean; no Super Bowl or World Series telecast to watch.

Back to the private sector and transparency - if you are recruited and accept a position that means moving from your home town of Port Judith, Rhode Island to Bend, Oregon the process should include telling you to pack your cowboy boots and Stetson hat and forget about four seasons and salt water breezes.

Recruitment starts the retention process. Retention of good people should be one of the objectives of any company. It must be one of the goals of anyone who desires to become a more effective manager. Unless the company is going through a right-sizing exercise or there is misconduct or negligence on the part of the employee, separation of an employee solely for the convenience of the company is normally, not always but normally a cop out on the part of the immediate supervisor – don't let it happen to you.

Why a cop out you might ask? There are a number of reasons – most of them excuses. An immediate supervisor may not have taken the time to mentor, coach or train a subordinate. Or take a real interest in her work. They may have been too pre-occupied with their own career goals or pre-occupied with micromanaging rather than in supervising.

Develop a sense of management based on fairness rather than equality or parity. I believe that many times, especially in the public sector organizations try to create an *artificial* work environment. One based on, in my opinion a false premise that the playing field is always level. It is not - This is the real work environment.

Bill Gates was reported to have told a high school graduating class that; "Life is not fair – get used to it." I fully agree with this. However, I'd like to add that as a more effective manager while life may not be fair, you can still try to put some fairness into it.

A friend of mine in Bolivia once said to me that the Constitution of the United States says that, "all men are created equal." I mentioned that although I was not around when this was being debated, I thought that this model had to do a lot with access to opportunities and rights. Equal access to opportunities in education, in the work place, etcetera; the right for everyone to exercise free speech and expression; and, equality in societal acceptance regardless of race, color, creed, age or whatnot. I also mentioned that although the Constitution said that all men are created equal, I saw no mention that they had to stay equal.

A concept so basic that it seems almost embarrassing to mention is that you, as a more effective manager must make people decisions based on merit and not biases or prejudices or misinformation received from others. You must also realize and understand that every employee may not be a workaholic or on the fast track or an over-achiever. Everyone does not want to be a supervisor or a corporate executive.

Let's look at electronic, information management systems (IMS) for a minute and their link with people. As programs involving financial management, results reporting and analysis, management of human resources or whatever become more available and incorporated into a more centralized corporate America, the need to recognize the importance of the human element in the equation is even more important. Why? – Because nothing can replace face to face communication. No matter how good the program is there will always be a need for clarifications or questions to be answered somewhere down the line. Those of you who may not be strong advocates of IMS must still recognize the value of their contribution to making an operation more efficient.

People design systems. People implement systems. People interpret systems output. People manage systems. More effective managers look for ways to balance systems output and the need for people to manage that output. We receive far too often, too many unsigned and impersonal letters or correspondence not only of the junk-mail variety, but as answers to our individual questions as well. From my point of view, systems designers should put more customer recognition into their design plans and their final software products.

What happens when there is no balance between people and electronic or mechanic collection systems and collection of data outpaces human resources capabilities? Lag time creeps in for one. Data keeps piling up. No one is available to look at it, or to interpret it. This affects many areas including national security.

I heard that several U.S. Government organizations were increasing the number of analysts to evaluate data that is being gathered from not only their sources but collected from other agencies as well. The common denominator in the success of any system is: people. The common denominator in the success of any organization or company is: people.

Reality check: More often than not, during the hiring phase organizations do not prepare new employees for the real work environment. And, far too many supervisors spend too little time mentoring subordinates and focusing on the retention of human resources. NOT GOOD.

SIXTH SENSE:

A More Effective Manager uses that God given "keen intuitive power", that sixth sense to help him manage.

This sense is very useful when we try to anticipate the reactions of others. Anticipation is the act of looking forward, or, to visualize a future event.

A wiser manager anticipates in the work environment as best as he can by utilizing actual indicators and/or his "gut feeling;" his "sixth sense." This is that subconscious ability that we all have that helps us to determine future reactions to things that we will do.

I knew a young, bright and ambitious USG personnel officer who took it upon herself to try to implement a major change in the completion of a performance evaluation form that was being used. Basically, the change was to have the form sent to the rater at the beginning of the rating cycle. The rater was asked to complete the section entitled "Goals and Objectives" for the upcoming rating period, discuss them with the employee and then to return the form to the personnel office. The block on the form indicated that this was mandatory for employees in grade levels *nine and above.*

In spite of this direction, the form was also sent to those supervisors rating employees in grade levels *eight and below* with instructions from her to also complete this action. Needless to say, the reaction from this group was very negative. While her intentions may have been good, the perception that she was creating additional work for those supervisors who rated employees in these lower grades led to disaster.

When we were discussing this her comment to me was, "Well, I had a feeling all along that this would happen." Although she anticipated a negative reaction, she did not try to lessen the effect that it would have on the raters (her customers) who had to do the work. One possible way to reduce this may have been to educate them beforehand or at least explained to them why she thought that what she was doing was in the best interests of both the employee and rater.

You can help yourself anticipate to a better degree if you develop knowledge of your customers - that market or group that will be affected by any decision that you make. Your gut feeling can be stimulated by a question such as; "I wonder what they'll think about . . .?" The answer being; "My gut feeling tells me that . . ."

I am not lessening the importance of the need to actively seek out information by soliciting feedback. This feedback, along with use of your sixth sense will go a long way in helping you to cut your losses and reduce your headaches. Reducing negative reactions will make your managing less complicated. Try not to create your own problems.

Use your sixth sense and anticipate.

Reality Check: Far too many times we under-utilize our sixth sense or gut feeling. NOT GOOD.

LEADERSHIP:

A More Effective Manger provides leadership.

He leads by example. He also understands that providing leadership is a continuous action. To lead is "to guide or conduct; hence, to direct in action, thought, opinion, etc; instruct." Leadership is simply the ability to lead.

What is a good leader? In my opinion this is too often measured, or judged by end results or popularity polls. I'll tell you what I believe makes an exceptionally good leader. Among his attributes are: use of good judgment; having patience, compassion, understanding and a sense of fairness; surrounding himself with competent advisors; knowing when to go against the grain or against conventional wisdom; and, knowing when to go with his gut feeling and using common sense.

I said that these are among his attributes. Don't forget skills in the art of negotiation and compromise, astute listening powers, a keen decision making process and, a dozen or so other attributes that you can list as a more effective manager.

Read this out loud, and listen to yourself carefully: "Effective management, let alone more effective management or being an exceptional leader is not a part-time job; neither is it that difficult." To manage more effectively takes focus, perseverance, a bit of luck and knowledge of the awareness elements mentioned herein.

Leadership is an integral part of being a better manager. On a more visible and more frequently seen plane are your attitude, work ethics and standards, appearance and dress, treatment of other people and your ability to stay calm, cool and collected under duress. These too contribute to your image as a leader.

Leaders are not born. They work at becoming leaders.

A leader has character. He is also a life long learner.

A leader is not afraid of challenges. My first full time military assignment was as a platoon leader with the 2nd Battalion, 15th Infantry, 3rd Division in Wildflecken, Germany. This was a mechanized Infantry unit. The only problem for me was that I was not an Infantry officer. I was in the Adjutant Generals Corps, detailed for two years to the Infantry. So what happened? The bastards assigned damn near every problem soldier in the battalion to me. I got the unit's "dirty dozen" to manage. The sons-of-bitches tried to set me up for failure.

Was this a challenge? You bet. End result. Six months later we were one of three platoons that passed a two-day training proficiency test; on the first try! The other eight or nine platoons had to retake it. After it was over I gave everyone in the platoon a one day pass and strolled into the Officer's Club, ordered myself a double CC on the rocks and came within a hairs' breath of telling the Infantry snobs to kiss my Ranger tab and Airborne wings. (Actually, we were a fairly close knit unit and I had some good friends there - one of whom made the ultimate sacrifice in Vietnam).

We will discuss empowering and delegating authority, but not responsibility later on. I'll mention it briefly now as it is important to understand when exercising your leadership role. When a leader empowers and delegates authority, he has to put limitations on the authority that he delegates.

How would you like a subordinate to announce as policy, a four-day work week? And when asked, "Why?" reply, "Hey man, I'm empowered to make decisions and I just made one." This may sound far-fetched, and it probably is, but – you get the point?

No matter how flat your organization is structured or how much rhetoric is being said about "empowerment" to employees, there must be leadership in an organization. If not, the organization could fall into disorder. Chaos could result. Employees and customers may become confused as to whom to direct questions to or, worse yet who is in charge. Empowerment of employees does not mean reneging on providing leadership. On the contrary, leadership becomes even more important.

Recognize that leadership starts at the top and that you are at the top of whatever organizational unit it is that you are managing. I have heard some people say that leadership begins at the bottom. Not so in my opinion. Think about it. Leadership – to lead is to be out in front, to set the pace and to have others follow your lead. It is called *leader*ship – *not follow*-ship.

Keep in mind that leadership is not about taking care of you, it is about taking care of others. While a Second Lieutenant serving in Germany one of the soldiers in the platoon that I led was a Korean veteran who held two Silver Stars for bravery along with his Combat Infantryman's Badge and other awards. He never rose above the rank of Sergeant E-5. He'd wind up screwin' up somehow and always get busted. He had a drinking problem to go along with his combat fatigue syndrome. He never caused any problems and carried more than his weight in field exercises and in the performance of day to day duties. The Army didn't kick him out – they (we) took care of him.

The concept of leadership is not new. We see it everywhere. In the family, who do the children look up to for guidance or to lead them through their growing pains? Is there shared leadership between mother and father? How about the leadership role of an older brother or sister? Does anyone provide the leadership needed to keep the family together?

In our schooling, does the teacher provide leadership in the classroom or the class president leadership to the class or the football captain leadership to the team?

In our government, who do the people look up too to lead them as a nation? The list goes on, and on, and on, and on.

There must be leadership in the work place. As a more effective manager it is incumbent upon you to provide that leadership. But remember, no leader works in a vacuum. Bring in others through empowerment and delegation of authority and utilization of other awareness elements to carry out your leadership role.

Reality check: Most people want to be led. Far fewer want to lead. Unfortunately, still too many managers fall into the first category. NOT GOOD.

OPTIONS AND DECISION MAKING:

A More Effective Manager looks at all of the options before making a decision.

The basic decision making process is valid. Define the problem; form a hypothesis; test the hypothesis; evaluate the test results; make a decision.

Regrettably, sometimes we tend to oversimplify the problem. This is especially true when a single solution seems obvious. *Contrary to what some management gurus may think, management is not an exact science.* What works in Washington may not work in New York, let alone in New Delhi. Indeed, what worked today may not work tomorrow.

I have always maintained, "Look both ways before crossing the street, even if it is crossing a one-way street." Sure enough, a friend of mine was in Mendoza, Argentina crossing a one-way street. You got it. He gets hit by a car that was backing up the one street! My friend looked up the street, which was the obvious thing to do, to see if any vehicles were coming down the one-way street. But, he forgot to look down the street; bad decision. The result was one broken leg and three weeks in the hospital.

An example that is hard for me to forget happened in the short class on squad tactics that I took at Fort Benning, Georgia. Close your eyes for a moment after reading this paragraph and picture this. Imagine a huge, 3-demensional terrain model on the stage in front of you. The model is complete with hilltops, buildings, trees, vegetation, streams, gullies, and ponds. Objective; capture Hill 402 located at the top of the terrain model and defended by a small enemy force.

The class was divided into five or six groups. What happened when it came time for each group to present their solution for capturing Hill 402? You guessed it; there were five or six different solutions. What was the instructor's reaction? He congratulated all teams for their work and said that every one of them had come up a possible solution. In this scenario, as in most cases the best solution would not been known until they were all tried.

We'll talk about end results as a measure of performance later. In the above scenario, we're talking about selecting the best option where the end result would mean the fewest number of deaths or casualties. We are not talking about an end result that will lead to bigger profit margins or to a more comfortable work environment. Both of which are important issues in the private sector, corporate world for sure.

How do you guarantee yourself or your colleagues that you selected or recommended the best solution if you haven't tried them all? You don't. In most cases you can't. You may not always have the luxury, or the time to test all of the possible solutions to a problem before making a final decision.

Then again, you must be reasonably assured that the course of action that you are recommending, or taking will succeed. You must have faith and trust in your own judgment. *Trust yourself.* Bring into play other awareness elements, such as anticipating. Before sticking your neck out as a minimum be sure to look at all of the options before making a final decision.

Having said all of this, don't let the obvious escape you. This example may sound like a personal matter but think about the work linkage. A friend of mine had to make a decision as to whom to invite to the Wednesday night poker game. The choices were the company president or a fellow co-worker. No need to sleep too long on this one, right? Pluses for inviting the president included additional exposure, in a more relaxed environment for someone who perceived himself as being on the fast track. A bonus plus; Mr. President wasn't a very good card player.

Unfortunately, the more options that we come up with the more difficult it may be to select one. You got it; we sometimes create our own dilemmas.

Reality check: Most managers do a decent job at looking at their options. GOOD.

COMMUNICATING - RELATING - WAITING:

A More Effective Manager communicates and relates without waiting.

This applies to communications with his superiors, subordinates, co-workers and any outside customers. What is communication? According to Mr. Webster it is a "process by which information is exchanged between individuals through a common system of symbols, signs, or behavior." Webster also goes on to point out that it is a "technique for expressing ideas effectively (as in speech)."

A more effective manager then should be able to communicate effectively both verbally and through written communications. Communicate the message that you want to get across in a clear and concise manner. Get to the point and cut the rhetoric. No gobbledygook or cockamamie stories. This will help to increase the recipients understanding of whatever it is that you are trying to communicate. If the communication is instructional in nature, mistakes will be minimized.

Communication must be timely. You cannot wait until the last minute to tell people what you want to say.

This gem was reinforced by an incident that happened to me while flying back to La Paz, Bolivia from Miami, Florida on the midnight red-eye special. It is one o'clock in the morning and I'm flicking the overhead reading light on and off every five or ten minutes to jot down some ideas for a project that I was working on.

I begin to notice that the guy behind me gives the back of my seat a little kick when I turn the light on. I start thinking to myself, what's wrong with that inconsiderate idiot behind me, he keeps kicking my seat. The guy behind me is thinking, what's wrong with that inconsiderate idiot in front of me, here it is one o'clock in the morning and he keeps turning the overhead reading light on and off every five or ten minutes.

Both of us are unhappy campers for the next hour or so. Why? Neither one of us communicated or related to the other in a timely manner. Heck, I didn't even try; I was on a project roll.

The guy behind me tried to communicate with me, but without success. Why? His method of telling me that he was unhappy with what I was doing was by kicking the back of my seat. This was an action that I did not relate to in a positive manner.

In fact, all it probably did, subconsciously, was to irritate me. It may have made me lose my concentration and, in the long run caused me to take more time than I may have needed to finish what I was doing. Notice how easy it is to, "shift the blame?" (We'll have more to discuss about shifting the blame in a later item).

Let me close this one with one more example. While it does not come from any of my experiences gained on the gridiron, on the battlefield or in the board-room it does illustrate how the misunderstanding of just one word can affect the outcome of a situation.

Picture this. It's my first day on my first real paying job, at age sixteen. I'm a kitchen helper in a large restaurant. Chores included dish and bottle washer and "go-fer." I looked up from what I was doing and saw the chef; Ester hunkered over four of five smoking frying pans. I ran over to her and asked if I could help. Sure she says, go into the other room and get "Earl." I run into the other room and no one is there. In walked a waiter and I asked him if he was Earl. He told me "no" so I ran back to Ester and told her I couldn't find Earl. Now, nearly hysterical she screamed at me, "Go back into the room, open the black door and get Earl."

I ran back into the room and opened the black door; it's a storage room filled with flour sacks, potatoes, cans of cooking oil, etc. Just then another waiter walks in and I ask him if he's Earl. He told me "no," put a big smile on face and walked away.

I ran back to Ester, who I could hardly see now through the billowing smoke and told her again that I couldn't find Earl. She was really pissed off now. She grabbed me by my sleeve, dragged me into the other room, opened the black door, pointed to the cooking oil and yelled "Earl, Earl."

Little did I know that Ester came from a small town in West Virginia where the town-folk pronounced "oil" like "Earl." Where I grew up, Earl was a man's name!

End result? I spent the next half hour or so scrapping burnt beans and as-paragus from the four or five frying pans. And, the waiter with the smile on his face who knew where Ester came from, had his laugh for the day.

Communication is essential to success. It is important to appreciate the need to keep the lines of communications flowing both vertically and horizontally. In the electronic age of E-mail it is fairly common to see multiple addressees as recipients. You have an option to delete or add folks. But don't overlook one thing; if you hit the wrong key and take your boss out of the loop, make sure that you bring him back in at some point.

For those of you out there who are chartists, remember that organization charts normally do not represent how people work in a highly successful or-ganization. They are not "operational" charts. They show which people report to whom. Unfortunately, they are often used as a tool to fix the blame (more on this later). A more effective manager knows that in the real world much of the way that we conduct business and manage falls on what we do and who we communicate with outside of the boxes. A somewhat dichotomy of chartists: they put people "in" the box while at the same time they want them to think "outside" of the box.

Effective communication sometimes jumps over boxes and solid and dotted vertical or horizontal lines. It also goes diagonally to those who may be uncon-nected on the chart!

Reality check: It seems like that the higher up that we get on the management ladder, the poorer our communications skills become with those on the lower rungs. NOT GOOD.

RISK TAKING:

A More Effective Manager is not afraid to take risks.

The environment we live in is not risk free. Neither is the work environment free of risk. On the international scene even the Dalai Lama recognizes risk. Among his good karma advice in 2005 -"Take into account that great love and great achievements involve great risk."

Risk in the intangible areas such as customer acceptance of a new product or employee acceptance of new dress standards or work hours are perhaps the most difficult to deal with. However, once the decision has been made to do something or to change something, you take the risk to implement.

I mentioned going back to Bolivia with one wife, three kids, one dog and one cat - and no job. I reduced my risk somewhat by having a general knowl-edge of Bolivia and her customs and traditions. I brushed up on my Spanish. I also made sure that I kept enough in the Korponai coffer to buy five return tickets to the good old U.S. of A. The dog and cat were expendable - at least to me.

My wife decided to change careers at age forty-nine. She went from teaching at the American Cooperative School (ACS) in La Paz to opening up her own pre-kindergarten. She became an owner, operator and manager. She lowered her risk of failure by mirroring her pre-kinder program after the one at the ACS.

Her school was conducted in the English language since her market study found that there was a real need for bilingual teaching at this level. The excellent reputation she acquired while teaching at the ACS for nearly thirteen years did not hurt either.

I firmly believe that people who are not afraid to take individual risk have greater potential to become more effective managers. Why? Because they tend to be good planners, anticipate well and basically, seem to balance risk with reasonableness. Do I really want to bungee jump? – If so, is the bungee cord tied securely around my ankles? How about the safety line?

Most risk takers and better managers tend to be more open minded and better listeners. You best listen carefully to all the pros and cons before risking that 10K in the stock market, or in a mutual fund, or in T-notes, or in precious metals or at the race track.

They are more apt to be self-starters and exhibit self-confidence. They more gamely challenge the existing status quo and are not afraid to rock the boat or to try to change the existing paradigm.

Although it may appear paradoxical, most risk takers are also team players. They are team players because in many cases, while they may be taking an individual risk they understand that others are involved in some phase of successful completion of that individual risk. You want to snowboard on that virgin snow on the top of Mount Everest? The helicopter pilot taking you up there is also taking a risk as he navigates through updrafts and swirling winds.

If you think that risk taking is not one of your strong areas, add a little "Pizzazz" to your life. A pinch of spice and a bit of risk taking never hurt anyone, even in the work environment.

Let me leave you with this anonymous piece that keeps popping up:

> *"To laugh is to risk appearing the fool.*
> *To weep is to risk appearing sentimental.*
> *To reach out for another is to risk involvement.*
> *To expose feelings is to risk exposing your true self.*
> *To place your ideas, your dreams before a crowd is to risk their loss.*
> *To love is to risk not being loved in return.*
> *To live is to risk dying.*
> *To hope is to risk despair.*
> *To try is to risk failure.*
> *But risks must be taken, because the greatest hazard in life is to risk nothing.*
> *The person who risks nothing does nothing, has nothing, and is nothing. They may avoid suffering and sorrow but they cannot learn, feel, change, grow, love, live. Chained by their certitudes they are a slave, they have forfeited their freedom.*
> *Only a person who risks is free."*

Too many managers are reluctant to take risk in the work environment. Notwithstanding this, we put our most precious possessions (ourselves and family members) on an airplane without even thinking to ask to see the latest crew or airplane certifications. Talk about taking a risk.

And, God forbid if something should go wrong what do we do? We fix the blame. Blame it on poor government oversight or control or airline mismanagement or pilot error. Regarding the former, at times I feel that we encourage Big Brother's participation and control and encroachment in our lives. We cannot have it both ways.

The desire for career stability and the "safety net" factor of retirement plans tends to stifle risk taking. Having just said that: there is nothing wrong with wanting a twenty or thirty year career with a company. What one must do is find some balance. Balance between acceptance of the status quo or challenging it. Identify and evaluate the professional and personal risks involved and decide what is best for you.

Along with risk taking is risk assessment. We do it everyday. It is a part of our daily lives and it's done consciously or sub-consciously. Crossing the street? You lower your risk by looking both ways. Risk assessment? You bet. Is the car coming down the street far enough away and going slow enough that you can cross the street safely.

For those of you who drive. When the light is yellow, do you try to run it or stop? Depending on the road conditions you may want to accelerate a bit and run it if the road is wet and slippery or icy. Slamming on the brakes may put you, and other drivers or pedestrians in more jeopardy if you enter into an uncontrollable skid.

An incorrect conclusion drawn from a risk assessment in the above driving scenario or in some shop or hazardous work environments may result in your injury or death. In the worse case scenario, an incorrect conclusion drawn from a risk assessment in the office environment could result in the loss of your job; but, you still have your life - and an opportunity to find another job.

Risk assessment – use it.

Reality Check: Most organizations could do with more risk takers at all levels. Not enough managers take it to the edge of the envelope. NOT GOOD.

SOLUTION TO EVERY PROBLEM - PERSISTENCE:

A More Effective Manager knows that no matter how impossible it seems or how hopeless the situation looks that there is a solution to every problem.

I was sitting in my office one day hearing an employee complain about how difficult it was for him to drive his vehicle into his driveway which was on a narrow, congested street. You're right, I'm up to my elbows in alligators so I am really only hearing what he has to say, and *not listening* to what he has to say.

In strolls Ernie Engineer who says "For a plate of Brazilian beans I'll solve your problem. Every problem has a solution." I begin to listen! He's right. Whether it can be solved by an engineering equation, by good old common sense or whatever, there is a solution.

Keep in mind however that your solution may not always meet with everyone's approval or have everyone's concurrence. It may not be viewed as a popular solution. And, God forbid, you may not have gotten a consensus.

A brief word about consensus - I have seen, far too often managers spend far too much time trying to make decisions by getting consensus. While consensus is a valid concept, the situation should dictate the selection of the solution process. *It is important for the more effective manager to select the best solution* whether it is made unilaterally or by consensus or by the flip of a coin.

Determination and persistency in finding a solution play an important role here. Do not confuse being persistent with being a pest. Someone who annoys is a pest. Someone who is persistent is determined and will find a solution to a problem.

President Calvin Coolidge, years ago summed this up very nicely when he said:

> *"Nothing in the world can take the place of persistence. Talent will not; nothing is more common than unsuccessful men with talent. Genius will not; unrewarded genius is almost a proverb. Education will not; the world is full of educated derelicts. Persistence and determination alone are omnipotent. The slogan 'Press On' has solved and always will solve the problems of the human race."*

You may want to bring into play other awareness elements in your search for a solution to a problem. Like what? -Brainstorming for one. Another is listening to feedback. If there is a central theme in problem solving, it is getting other people involved (We'll talk about synergism in a later awareness element).

A real problem for the S.J. Groves & Sons Company in Bolivia was civil suits being brought against them by local residents living along the route of the new road being built. Many had claimed that their property was damaged or destroyed during the construction of the road. Despite the fact that we had a local attorney, his forte was corporate, not civil law. I was spending an excessive amount of time in the local court house on these matters pleading the company's cases before a local judge. Finally I suggested to the Project Manager that we hire not only a local attorney versed in civil law, but, now get this, that we hire, not bribe but hire the judge who was presiding over our cases! He bought it and we hired her away from the court. Was this the solution to our problem? You bet. We got an experienced attorney who not only knew the law, but one who knew the system as well.

Again, bear in mind that the easiest and most likely solution to your problem may not be the one to take. But also keep in mind that you may not need a complicated solution to solve a complicate problem either. In any case, don't give up. There is a solution to every problem.

And remember that there may be more than one solution to a problem. Identifying multiple solutions can lead to a problem in itself; procrastination in decision making.

Reality Check: Too many managers are reluctant to offer solutions that may be viewed as "unpopular" or that have not gone through a consensus process. NOT GOOD.

FEEDBACK; POSITIVE AND NEGATIVE:

A More Effective Manager listens to both positive and negative feedback.

Positive feedback tells us what our customers like about us and the way that we are doing business. This gives us confidence by letting us know that we are going in the right direction.

Negative feedback tells us what our customers do no like about us. It normally puts us in a reaction mode. On the other hand, negative feedback may also give us direction in our search for other options or solutions to problems. An alternative course of action may result.

Negative feedback can also lead us to the source of a larger problem. An example of this was seen in the tragic AMTRACK accident that happened in the 1990's. I believe that an investigation and interviews (feedback) led to the conclusion that the engineer may have ingested a foreign substance before or during the trip. Further inquires found that there may have been wide-spread substance abuse among AMTRACK employees. AMTRACK officials listened and, if I remember correctly, took corrective actions that included instituting a program of random drug testing of employees for substance use.

Negative feedback can lead to better morale if we listen to it and take some action. While working with S.J. Groves & Sons in Bolivia one of the Bolivian site workers, who at one time numbered nearly 300 had the courage to criticize (negative feedback) what was being served for breakfast.

What was being served for breakfast? We served eggs, ham, bacon, toast, hash browns, cereal, milk, fresh fruit, tea and coffee; sounded damn good to me. What we "gringo" foreigners forgot to consider was the culture that we were working in: The Bolivian worker was used to soup, bread, cheese and strong coffee for breakfast. Result? These were added to the breakfast table. They got what they wanted and what they were accustomed to eating. Result? We had 300 happier campers.

Don't forget to solicit feedback (information). Ask questions or send out questionnaires, or whatever. Soliciting feedback will show others that you have an interest in their well-being and in the company's success.

Let's complete the cycle. Once you've solicited feedback and have processed the results; share the results. This will lead to customer confidence and trust. You may want to share this information with other departments or units in the company. There may be some cross-cutting areas that will be of some help or assistance to others within the company.

Here are a few last thoughts about negative feedback. Negative feedback is just as important as that pat on the back. *Don't be afraid of negative feedback.* Learn from it and turn it into a positive, proactive rather than reactive action. Taking a proactive role from negative feedback will let employees and customers know that you listen and that you are not afraid to change or to try to improve or better an existing situation.

If you do receive negative customer feedback don't fall into the trap of spending eighty percent of your time on five percent of your problems. Case in point - Right around 1993 – 1994 we designed and conducted a customer satisfaction survey of General Services in Cairo. These included the warehouse, motor pool, residential maintenance, operation of the cafeteria and custodial services (There may have been two or three more). The results of the eighty or so surveys received from the American employees were along the following lines: 3 F's; 7 or 8 D's; 25 or so C's; 30 or so B's; and, about 15 A's. The normal Bell-shaped distribution curve was skewed to the positive.

When discussing the results with some senior managers one of them made the comment to me of: "Well Dave you now know where you have to put some extra effort." When I asked "Where?" he said; "Ya gotta get those F's off of the report card – they don't look good."

My response was that if we were going to make any additional efforts it would be to keep the A's and B's from slipping into a lower bracket and to get the C's and D's into a higher bracket. We wouldn't write off the F's as they were still our customers. In my opinion they would go on to realize the better than average quality support that they were getting, after they left the Mission.

At the grass-roots level a more effective manager distinguishes those customers who are the chronic complainers and whiners from those who may offer negative feedback and constructive criticism to go along with it. Some folks will find fault and bitch or complain or whine about something even if they were living in the Taj Mahal and being serviced by JC and the boys.

When asking for feedback, keep in mind that you may not always hear the answer that you want to hear. The bottom line is, "If you don't want the feedback, don't ask the question."

If you're someone who takes negative feedback personally, then maybe this is a weakness that you should work on improving. We'll focus on identifying one's strengths and weaknesses as a piece of the puzzle later on.

Recap: Think of soliciting feedback as a means of gathering information; and, then sharing the information with your customers. This should lead to a better understanding of customer expectations. Please don't forget that the customers include the employees whom you supervise. You are a more effective manager now. Take that negative feedback and turn it into a positive.

Reality Check: In spite of what we can learn from feedback, too many managers are still reluctant to ask for it, primarily because they are afraid of getting "negative" feedback. NOT GOOD.

TAKING A REAL INTEREST IN SUBORDINATES:

A More Effective Manager takes a real interest in subordinates.

Does this mean that you have to know a subordinates' job? Hell no. But, it may help in some cases. The old paradigm was that a manager had to be able to do her subordinate's job.

Now there is just too much specialization. It is damn near impossible to know the particulars of all of the components of everyone's job. Showing an interest in his work, rolling up your sleeves to help him, and showing that you care about his work, his work environment and his working conditions is what this is all about.

Don't forget to listen to what he has to say. Include an interest in his career development and training and you have a more complete picture of this.

Maintaining your interest in underlings is just as important. Regardless of your management position, this can mean walking through the work area. Some people call this - Management by Walking Around.

Scheduled or impromptu staff meetings or meetings with individuals or small groups should not be overlooked. These may be good times to share information of common interest and to listen to feedback.

When I accepted a new position within the same agency that I worked for it meant moving to a different building that was eight or ten blocks away from my old office. Notwithstanding the fact that I was wearing "two hats" and part of my responsibilities included supervision over the office that I had left, I still made it a point to show a physical presence there at least 3 or 4 times a month.

On a lighter side, make sure that the flickering florescent tube over Mike Messenger's desk gets replaced and that there's enough toilet paper in the crapper.

Taking an interest in and getting to know the people whom you supervise could also have some effect, positive I hope on their personal as well as professional life. You may be able to identify a gambling, drinking or substance abuse problem. If you do; what then? Switch hats? Take off the "Supervisor" hat and put on the "I'm Your Friend" cap, or clergy collar! Confront and counsel the person as both a supervisor and a friend. However, remember that a more effective manager knows when to back off when engaging in personal issues with a subordinate or with other co-workers. Most important of all, respect the fact that most people believe, and rightfully so that they have both a professional and private life.

We can probably come up with a number of other questions and scenarios. Whatever you do, call on some of the other awareness elements; evaluate the situation and circumstances and use your common sense.

Take a real interest in your subordinates. They are your customers as well.

Reality Check: Most employees come to work because they have to, not because the want to. (NOT GOOD) Taking a real interest in them can help turn this around and most of the managers I know do a decent job at this. GOOD.

IF IT AIN'T BROKE, DON'T FIX IT:

A More Effective Manager knows that if it ain't broke, it don't need fixin'.

I know that I mentioned earlier that a more effective manager is not afraid of change, and that she should, in fact seek ways to improve operations through change. That's still a given.

Keep in mind that one should not make a change solely for the sake of change. There must be a reason for a change. The philosophy should be that change must have a positive effect on something. The change may lead to a better product, to better customer services, to a better work environment, to improved worker morale or to a better way of doing business. Hopefully a change will also make tasks easier for some, or all employees.

More effective management requires that you give serious thought and evaluation to proposed changes. Will the new office paint job have a positive effect on employee morale? How about the day care center for workers with pre-school aged children? What effect will the new vending machine and the new furniture in the customer waiting area have on your customers? How about the plants for the office? Do you implement flex-time to solve chronic worker tardiness?

Try to visualize the effect of a change. This goes along with using your sixth-sense. Close your eyes and visualize how the changes in the customer's waiting area will look or how those soft, cool, pastel greens or blues will look on the walls of the offices.

In a business sense, what we are asking is, "What is going to be the return on our investment if we make a change, or changes?" That's right. Normally *change is going to cost something.* It could mean an increased financial cost; either up front or long term. If so, how much and how long will it take to recover costs? It could also "cost" the company its image with its employees or customers.

Years ago ESSO, a large oil company changed their name. They draped their signs with covers that read; "What's come over the ESSO sign." Neat advertising gimmick – keep the public guessing – cost to whet customer imagination - practically nothing.

If you play a key role in bringing about a change it could also cost you in the way people will see you as the innovator or supporter of that change. Are you advocating for the change to butter up the boss or to kiss his ass? Or, are you pushing for the change because it really is in the best interests of your section or the company?

Whether they are your ideas or someone else's, you've got to look at proposed changes as objectively as possible. An organization that I knew operating overseas was loaning a large tent that it owned to the British Embassy. The Brits had been requesting the use of this tent for the past five years, for the Queen's Birthday celebration hosted by the British ambassador.

This was literally no cost to the organization. The set up and take down time of the tent was not more than a total of two hours, done by local salaried employees. Since many dignitaries including the American ambassador attended this function, the public relations image as an organization that participated in and cared about intercultural activities was greatly enhanced by the loan of this tent to the British Embassy.

Along comes a new section chief and change. "We will not make the tent available to the Brits from this day on!" No questions were asked such as; "Why are we doing this?" "How long have we been doing this?" "What effect will this have on community relationships?" The impression that I got was along the lines of change for the sake of change only.

What this brings up is a need to understand the pendulum swing that may be brought about by a new chief. In a lot of scenarios a new manager, a new Colonel, a new General or a new Director will want to leave their mark on the organization; especially if the position is viewed by them as a stepping stone to a promotion. Nothing wrong with that unless it becomes a quest or obsession based solely on personal rather than professional reasons. As a more effective manager on a lower rung on the organizational chart, keep in mind that situations like this are normally temporary. What the wiser manager takes away from this is an understanding that what the pendulum swing of change normally does is: leave something positive behind. Something that he may be able to build on.

If you believe that a change will make a difference in something in a positive way then go for it. If not, why try to change it? *However, always look for ways to make things better.*

Fine tuning and tweaking existing operational systems is like performing preventative maintenance or upgrading your vehicle. You probably don't buy a new car every year yet you might consider adding a stereo system or tinted glass to the old clunker.

Smarter managers continuously look for ways to improve morale, working conditions and relationships with the staff that he supervises. An old colonel gave me some wise counsel many years ago. He told me that if you can't take care of your own troops (employees), how can you expect them to take care of others?

Don't wait for things to become broken before you take actions to make them better. On the other hand, don't forget, if it ain't broke, don't fix it.

Reality Check: I genuinely agree that most managers advocate change for the betterment of the organization rather than for personal gain or attention. GOOD.

DEVELOPING SUBORDINATES:

A More Effective Manager develops subordinates.

Developing your subordinates should help improve the atmosphere in the work place, boost employee morale and improve the way that the unit conducts itself and it's business. Keep in mind that we spend a hellava lot of time in the work place. At least eight hours per day, Monday through Friday, 48 to 50 weeks per year.

There are many tools around that can help you develop subordinates. Getting someone enrolled in a training program is the most visible.

One of the most overlooked and underutilized means is a cross-training program within the organization. I have been in organizations where cross-training has reached out to train drivers to become procurement agents, carpenters to become upholsters and personnel specialists to become contracting specialists. Cross-training is also a very very very cost effective device.

How you develop subordinates and mold them together into a team in your work environment could be critical at some point in time in your operation. *The end result should be a more intelligent and informed work force.* One that leads to a better operation that will run more smoothly, like that well oiled machine.

You may have to devote some of your managing time to developing subordinates. Mentoring is the name of the game. Blocking out a part of your day or week for this may be necessary. Providing counsel and guidance to your subordinates is a sign of good leadership. Once again, you see some connectivity between various pieces of the puzzle.

I mentioned earlier but it is worth repeating. I have seen to often supervisors, especially those on the fast track renege on their role as a mentor. The excuse is oftentimes based on – I do have the time. But if they took some time from their own self-serving interests, they'd have the time.

Along these lines, developing employees will help create an atmosphere in the work environment to the extent that the people whom you manage will feel that they work *with you and not, for you.* Developing your subordinates will create an attractive, satisfying, and productive work environment which will make your managing less difficult and less complicated.

The more comfortable you feel with the players on the team that you lead, the sooner more positive results will be seen. Developing people will lead to this extended comfort zone.

Another real positive effect of a good training program is that it may make the employee a stronger candidate for a promotion. I am a strong advocate of promotion from within an organization. If someone is qualified to move into a vacancy that may mean a promotion, or a lateral transfer into a similar position in a different division or section they should be given preference. Support it and be prepared to lock horns with your EEO omnibus.

Remember, as a more effective manager keep the process of identification of employees for training professional, not personal. No favoritism to bowling buddies or friends.

A comment about deputies or assistants is in order. A more effective manager understands that a deputy or assistant manager plays a noteworthy role in the management process. He appreciates the balance that they bring to the workforce. They are oftentimes the buffer between the boss and customers and clients.

Deputies are more than just an extra pair of eyes and ears. In many cases it is the deputy who takes care of the daily operations while the boss is focusing on the bigger picture items that may be on the agenda. Experience gained as a deputy and mentoring from your boss go a long way in career development.

You and your deputy are: you got it, a team. Suffice to say now that a better manager realizes this which allows both of you to feed off of one another. Individual strengths are optimized. Individual weaknesses are minimized by the others strengths. The "good cop - bad cop" approach to balancing strengths and weaknesses will come natural with no rehearsals needed.

Reality Check: More often than not we simply do not spend enough time mentoring and developing subordinates. NOT GOOD.

MICROMANAGING:

A More Effective Manager does not micro-manage.

Micromanagement in this framework means not only telling subordinates what has to be done, but telling them how to do it as well. Micromanagement stifles creativity. You've got to develop subordinates in such a way that you have confidence in what they do. You know what their strengths are and what their weaknesses and limitations are.

You should try to keep the decision making process at the lowest level possible. Delegate authority! Remember however, you can delegate authority, but you cannot delegate responsibility. What does this mean? Here's what it means to me.

Authority is the power to make decisions that influence or control a person's thought, opinion or behavior. Responsibility is the quality or state of being responsible. Can an irresponsible person be in a position of authority? Of course, why not? Every employee should be responsible and, in any case must be held accountable for their actions whether they involve making decisions or not.

A manager's responsibility goes beyond only being responsible for his individual actions. To me a managers' responsibility includes being held accountable for his actions and, to a degree the actions of subordinates as well. It may sound like an old fashioned concept but, believe me it works.

Developing this attitude will help you to keep focused on what is going on in the work place. At the same time it will help prevent you from being viewed as a supervisor who has delegated absolute authority and all responsibility and can now, "wash his hands" of the matter - especially, if something goes wrong.

A more effective manager does not delegate and then disengage. He must remain involved in the process or activity that he has delegated. In the real world, there are very few instances of absolute delegation of authority. A good thing to remember: Everyone knows *how* to delegate; a more effective manager knows *when* to delegate.

And also remember that everything is easy, especially if you don't have to do it yourself. Keep an eye open to staff burnout if you delegate and then disengage, delegate and then disengage, delegate and then disengage adnauseam. As a wiser manager, don't fall into this trap.

Share your ideas and concepts and work philosophies with the people in the work force that you manage. Everyone should become a part of your team. Give them the leadership that they need to get the job done. Whenever possible, give them the ball and let them run with it. They will feel more appreciated. You will soon see how much more extra effort *involved* employees will voluntarily put into their work.

Bear in mind however, you should not over simplify and only trust menial tasks to employees. They must be given meaningful duties to perform. This is what empowering is all about. Knowledge of your workforce is imperative. It is even more important for those mangers who may be in a highly mobile work force; i.e. Project Managers, people in the military, etcetera. You have to tap into those employees with the institutional memory right?

I once managed a large General Services Office (GSO). The composition of this workforce included eleven drivers, ten white-collar clerk/secretarial employees, two mid-level managers and thirty-one blue collar tradesmen/laborers. I got to know them all better by, "Management by Walking Around."

We conducted a closed-bid sale one time that generated thousands of dollars for the United States Government. Hundreds of bids were received for 140 groups of items. My guidance to the employee I delegated with the authority to organize and conduct the sale was to identify items to be sold, arrange them in attractive groupings, prepare the advertisement, conduct the sale, account for bids and identify the highest bidder (the collection of monies was the responsibility of another office).

Jointly we established our operating "window" and developed our plan and strategy. My follow up actions included one or two meetings to solicit feedback on how things were progressing. I showed a physical presence during the selection of the items to be sold and at the sale itself. I was also present when the bids were opened.

The sale went off with nary a hitch. The agency participants from the GSO staff who where involved in some phase of the sale included one of the two mid-level managers, five of the clerk/secretarial employees and eight of the blue collar tradesmen/laborers and me. *We were all shareholders in this particular project.*

Giving people guidance and following up on that guidance is not micromanaging. Neither is offering suggestions. These are ways of developing employees. Walking through a shop area is not micromanaging. It shows that you take a real interest in your subordinates.

For whatever reason, the smaller the organization is the more likely it is to fall prey to micro-managing. Why? I don't have the complete answer to this one. One reason may be is that the manager may also be the owner and has a personal stake in the company; i.e. capital tied up in it and therefore wants to be involved in everyday decisions - Nothing wrong with that. Another may be that the organization is running smoothly, everyone knows and is doing their job and the manager winds up with too much free time on his hands. He's bored out of his gourd. Or, if things are going so well without his participation he feels threatened that his job may be in jeopardy. Or, he is on a fast track and wants to leave his mark prior to moving on.

Be careful, watch your micromanagement.

Reality Check: As a rule, supervisors who are workaholics, on the fast track or over-achievers are more apt to be micro-managers. Most of them simply do not have the patience to wait for others to finish a task, especially if it is not being carried out in way that they would do it themselves. NOT GOOD.

IS EVERYTHING IMPORTANT?:

A More Effective Manager understands that although everything that he does is important, some things are more important than others.

There is just not enough time in the work day to focus on all of the issues that you may have to face. You must be able to develop the ability to identify the issues or tasks that you want to address during the day or the week, recognize that they are all important to finish and then prioritize them.

Some are put on the "back burner" or "on hold". For how long is your decision based on your continuous evaluation of, among other things; short and long range goals and objectives, current human and material resources, budget, effect on employee morale, health or safety issues and the impact on customer relations or services.

I know an outstanding manager who became even better after visiting a management psychologist. He had developed a two page list of things to do and was getting frustrated as the list got longer and longer as new, unfinished "things" were added to it. The psychologist's advise: "Get rid of the damn list. Things that are important, that really need to get done will get done." Good advice? It was for this manager.

Don't get a coronary over this one folks, especially if you are the one setting the priorities. Why? -Because you are going to set realistic goals and objects for yourself and staff. You are not going to put too much on your plate at one time. You are also going to put things in proper perspective and balance.

Above all, you are going to prioritize your own work and help those whom you supervise so that all of you can have some time for your families and friends. I think that it was either Vince Lombardi, the ex-football coach of the Green Bay Packers or Knute Rockne, the ex-football coach at Notre Dame who said that the three most important things in a person's life are: 1. His God; 2. His family; and, 3. His work. It may have been: 1. His family; 2. His God, and 3. His work. In any case, work was in third place. We should all be able to learn and gain a little something from this.

Someone recently mentioned to me that he feels that he spends ninety per cent of his time on ten per cent of the issues that he has to deal with. Maybe this is so. If that's the case, then it is even more important that he organize himself and the people he manages by prioritizing tasks based on his evaluation of what the most important things are that he wants to accomplish. This will help to ensure optimum productivity from the human resources with whom he has to work with or manage.

When I was assigned to the Armed Forces Entrance and Examining Station in Newark, New Jersey our chief medical officer was an elderly retired colonel who had served in the tail end of World War I and in World War II. The commander of the station, a Lieutenant Colonel and West Point graduate we called Jumpin' Joe, was always pressing and pressuring the doctor to speed up the physical examinations.

One day the old Doc said, "Colonel, what do you want me to do first, look up someone's nose or look up his ass? I can't do both at the same time!" Both were an important part of the physical examination. The doctor decided that the nose would be first. Jumpin' Joe never bugged or bothered him again. Everything is important to someone.

Reality Check: Too many supervisors only do a mediocre job of prioritizing works. Because of it they spend far too much extra time in the office or on the job and too little time with their family and friends. NOT GOOD.

THE LEARNING PROCESS:

A More Effective Manager recognizes and understands the fact that the learning process never stops.

It never stops because (and swallow some of your pride you know-it-alls), people can always learn something more. It may be something more about their work, their hobby, other people or even themselves. The human brain has unlimited capacity.

Outstanding managers also recognize the value of learning not only from their supervisors but from subordinates, peers and customers as well. Learning from subordinates is an important concept that all of us at times tend to forget. There is probably a wealth of knowledge in your work environment. Knowledge to be gained from that old geezer sitting in the corner hunched over his desk to the new employee in the mini-skirt or Pierre Cardin tie who reeks with energy, and new ideas - tap into it.

Speaking of old geezers, the longer you stay in an organization you may want to think about what Edward Hersey Richards had to say:

> *"A wise old owl sat on an oak,*
> *The more he saw the less he spoke;*
> *The less he spoke the more he heard;*
> *Why aren't we like that wise old bird?"*

A more effective manager is not only a teacher or mentor, but he is a student as well. Learn to identify your learning resources. Call upon all of your senses to learn about what is going on around you.

A vital concept to keep in mind is that if you are selected to be a group or team leader, leaders are also learners. You got it. You have to learn about your team members. Assess their individual strengths, weaknesses and capabilities to function as a part of the team.

Most important, learn from your failures as much as you learn from your successes. Don't be afraid to make mistakes. "If you don't make mistakes, you aren't learning" as someone once mentioned to me. Learn from your mistakes and the mistakes of others also.

And for you materialists, the more you learn, the more you earn!

No matter what, don't ever forget that it's never too late to learn and that you're never too old to learn. An old dog can learn new tricks. The learning process never stops; we are always on the upward slope of the learning curve.

I think it was George Burns, who at age ninety said; "I learned that I still have a lot to learn."

Finally Mark Twain: "When I was a boy of fourteen, my father was so ignorant I could hardly stand to have the old man around. When I got to be twenty-one I was astonished at how much the old man had learned in seven years."

Reality Check: There are still too many senior managers out there who think that they know it all and, worse yet think that they can do the incumbent's job better than the incumbent can. NOT GOOD.

FOCUS, FOCUS, FOCUS:

A More Effective Manager focuses.

He focuses on the issue or the problem by screening out the nonessentials. This is probably one of the most difficult skills for a manager to develop.

In the real estate world the three most important words are; Location, location, location. In the ever changing, multi-dimensional real world of managing the battle cry is: Focus, focus, focus.

While focusing on the issue or the problem, you've got to avoid developing "tunnel vision." Keep an open mind in your quest to solve, or resolve problems.

USAID, and most other US government and military, and international organizations have an assigned housing policy. Prior to an employee coming to an overseas location a leased house or apartment is assigned to them. I once attended a housing board meeting where one of the issues centered on a discussion about implementing a mandated leased housing policy in the most cost effective manner. This entailed establishing a housing portfolio and assigning employees to housing units that were in this inventory of houses and apartments.

One board member kept emphasizing and stressing the need to stay within established size parameters that were based on the employees' position grade and family size. He failed to realize that the policy was developed to allow for a more flexible housing program where the real issue was establishing, maintaining and *managing* a cost effective program where the size of the residence was only one factor to consider.

In addition to the position grade of the employee and the size of his family, other factors to consider were ages and sexes of children, proximity to a school, special family needs, projected staffing levels, terms and cost of the lease agreement, projected maintenance costs, etcetera.

We spent nearly one-half hour listening to this guy talk about the size of kitchens and living rooms before my boss and I graciously excused ourselves from the meeting. Why did it take us that long? Good question. What we extended to this myopic manager was what I like to call, "professional courtesy."

I was on a steering committee that was tasked with coming up with a new organizational structure that would lead to a more efficient operation. Great idea, there is always room for improvement right? We met two or three times a week. We spent the first two or three weeks discussing, trying to define and making and revising lists of the detailed end results we expected from the new organization.

Seeing that we were going nowhere, one of the members recommended that we put aside the list of expectations. He suggested that we focus on trying to come up with a recommended organizational structure that would meet these, and any other's that may be added later. We refocused on the overall objective of recommending a different organizational structure that would lead to a more efficient operation.

We formed three working groups. We discussed and showed each one of them the wish list of expectations that was developed up to this point. We also discussed the main objective of trying to establish a more efficient operation.

Group one was asked to focus on tweaking and fine tuning the existing organization. Kind of like a mini, time and motion study. Add an additional messenger or whatever. How can the current structure be made even better or more functional without a real "real" reorganization?

Group three was asked to go wild and put on their creative thinking caps. Replace the director and deputy director with a troika; redefine "senior staff"; eliminate operational units; etcetera.

Group two was asked to take a look at modifying the existing organization. For example, roll existing operational units, with similar functions into one another; i.e. form teams based on objectives rather than technical specialties or look at reorganizing exiting committees. Basically, to come up with something between Group one and Group three.

In retrospect, what happened during those first two to three weeks was that the steering committee lost focus. It became too one-dimensional by focusing only on end result expectations. All of which were the desired outcome of any organization regardless of the structure. The list we made on day one, continued to get longer and longer as the sessions dragged on. We lost sight of the *big* picture.

Be as objective and creative as you can in resolving an issue or a problem while keeping the big picture in mind. Develop and adhere to a clear and concise agenda that focuses on the issue or problem.

Reality Check: It is a hellava lot easier to lose focus than it is to stay focused; therefore, still too many managers lose focus. NOT GOOD.

TUNING OUT TO TUNE IN:

A more effective manager listens.

He listens to the answers to the questions that he has asked. He also listens to comments, suggestions, recommendations, employee gripes, etcetera, etcetera, etcetera. He listens to everyone; customers, subordinates and superiors. He listens to everything. "Keep your ear to the ground", as the old saying goes.

Don't confuse hearing with listening. "I heard what he said" is not the same as "I listened to what he said." Why? Because we hear everything, from the spoken words of people to the background noises of slamming doors, air conditioners, radios or whatnot.

Take heed, hearing is the physical sense by which noises and tones are received as stimuli. Listening is focusing in on what is being said and paying attention to what is being said by filtering out background noises and distractions.

Active listening is what this is all about. Active listening also involves *processing* what is being said and learning from whatever it is that you are listening to.

Years ago my brother-in-law and I decided to take a risk and get into a business that neither one of us knew anything about. We got in touch with someone from a retired executive program. The acronym was SCORE, Service Corps of Retired Executives I believe. Unfortunately, we only heard what this guy had to say and we did not listen to what he had to say. We bellied up in about eighteen months.

Listening carefully can help you avoid being manipulated by words. I recently heard an exchange between a newscaster and a U.S. official in Iraq. It went something like this:

> *U.S. official: I believe that the Syrians and Iranians can cooperate more.*

> *Newscaster: Are you saying that the Syrians and Iranians are NOT cooperating?*

Hello. This is hearing, not listening. To me, this is also questionable reporting. The U.S. official did not say that there was no cooperation between the two countries. He said that there could be more (and hopefully better) cooperation between the two. As a more effective manager, don't let people put words in your mouth.

It is not that difficult. What you do with what you've listened to, is another matter. In any event, be a good listener and focus on whatever is being said.

Reality Check: Most people are not very good listeners. NOT GOOD.

ROCKING THE BOAT:

A More Effective Manager is not afraid to rock the boat, even if it means that he might fall into the water.

This could be an exciting area as rocking the boat usually means challenging something, or God forbid challenging someone, like your supervisor.

I had a nice, neatly groomed and rather lengthy, waxed handlebar mustache once that a general asked me to shave off because in his words it was, "against the regulations." So, sure enough I checked the regulation. It read something similar to "a mustache could not drop below the corners of the mouth." It did not however, restrict how far past the corners of the mouth that a mustache could go.

I wrote the proponent of the regulation. The regulation was changed to read something along the lines of, "the mustache cannot drop below the corners of the mouth and the length cannot go beyond an imaginary line drawn perpendicular from the corners of the eye." The result of my query (and possibly other's) was the establishment of a clear, well defined policy. Everyone was singing off the same sheet of music.

Rocking the boat can lead to what some management gurus refer to as a "paradigm shift"... a change to the existing model or pattern; doing something differently. This could become a sensitive and emotional issue.

There are organizations that I am familiar with that hire "retirees" to fill position vacancies within the organization. Most of the retirees fill a position vacancy similar to, or fill the same one that they were retired from. To me it sounds a little like double dipping. The argument is, "Look at all the experience that we are able to tap into." If that's the case, why retire the individual in the first place?

Let me play the devil's advocate here and look at what really happens. By hiring retirees, the organization is not tapping into the pool of new, though not necessarily young employees who can fill these positions. The "new blood", fresh talent and ideas are drying up.

Can retirees play an important role in these organizations? Of course they can. However, the trade off between hiring retirees and new employees needs to be looked at and evaluated very carefully.

Perhaps a paradigm shift is in order. Hire retirees to fill vacancies only at certain grade levels or at certain locations or in certain specialties. Look at hiring them at certain critical times such as during a start-up or closure or relocation. How about as a trainer?

How about hiring him at a reduced salary or without certain benefits. Let's be a little creative here for a minute. Since the monies are coming out of the same coffers, why not hire him at a percentage difference between the advertised salary and his retirement pay. This would still provide an incentive to the retiree to return to the manpower pool. Let's be even more creative and say that only a certain percentage of the adjustment would be taxable. How about allowing a retired employee to accumulate additional creditable retirement years (one for every two additional years of employment?) while not drawing his annuity during his "reemployment."

Is this discriminatory or unfair? Not to me. Selective use of a manpower pool of retirees is not discriminatory. It should be viewed as a privilege to come out of retirement to fill a vacancy in the same organization, or the same company. It should not be viewed as a right.

Let's take a shot at one more. The United States military is by far the most professional and effective military in the world. It maintains this status despite a policy that allows for voluntary retirement after twenty years of service and dictates mandatory retirement after thirty years of service, rare exceptions permitted.

Why not take a look at something along these lines for elected officials? Let's "rock the boat" and take on Congress.

Retirement information of elected "members" of Congress is contained in Title 5, United States Code Annotated. The code addresses mandatory separation at age seventy for all federal employees. However, it does not apply to a "member" of Congress. Why not? Good question!

A "member" can also draw an annuity at age 62, after serving only five years.

A member of the Armed Forces must serve a minimum of twenty years to draw any retirement benefits.

A military member on a two-term enlistment could have between five and six years of service after the completion of his second enlistment. During this time he could have had two tours of duty in Vietnam, Afghanistan or Iraq getting his ass shot at. He could have been assigned to any number of other hardship areas. When G.I. Joe gets out after six years he gets nothing; squat, nada, zero.

When Mr. Smith goes to Washington and then goes home after spending six years as a Congressman and maybe living in one of the more costly suburbs of Washington, and accessing stylish clubs and fitness centers, he leaves knowing he will get 10.5 percent (1.75 percent per year) of his average pay, at age sixty-two. Go figure!

While Congress attempts to micro manage agencies and departments within the federal government, to micro manage areas such as foreign affairs and welfare, to create humongous department's ala the plan to create a super Department of State and to "reinvent" government, it seems to me that they should also be looking at ways to make their legislative body more efficient. Cost driven changes should not be only relegated to lower echelons and affect only those on the lower rungs of the ladder.

One way is to get its personnel policies in line with other federal agencies. One of the areas that may need revamping is Title 5 "member" benefits. Congressional benefits cost the American taxpayer millions of dollars a year, period.

If you find yourself in a position where you keep hearing (or find yourself believing) that; "The company won't let it happen" or "The organization doesn't allow for things like this"; refocus. If in fact it can't happen maybe, just maybe it is because supervisors or employees like you, or me won't question or challenge the way that things are being done. You and other employees *are* the company or organization. It's people (us) who too often don't try to make it happen.

The point is; is it time to rock the boat, to challenge or to try to change a paradigm? There are other scenarios that we can continue to discuss but, let's stop the insanity right now.

Jack Welch, the former CEO of General Electric encouraged employees to challenge the decision making process. In some circles he is considered the most innovative executive of the 20th century. In my opinion a large part of this is due to his encouragement of employees to challenge management decisions – to "rock the boat."

Reality Check: Too many managers are content in what they do and, for whatever reason are not inclined to "rock the boat" or to challenge authority. NOT GOOD.

INTERACTION AND INTERPERSONAL SKILLS:

A More Effective Manager knows that interpersonal skills play an important role in interacting with people.

The United States Army, in the 1960's had a slogan posted on bulletin boards - *"Put the 'Personal' Back into Personnel."* This meant that individuals involved in personnel processing or personnel matters or issues, at any level in the command were to develop a "one-on-one" personal relationship with the soldiers (customers) whom they were serving. It didn't matter whether you were a sergeant helping a private or a colonel, or an officer helping an enlisted man or another officer. This one-on-one approach not only demanded but tested one's interpersonal skills.

What mattered was that you treated your customer, whoever he might be in a fair and professional manner. The "personal" touch better allowed for educating the customer, soliciting feedback and solving problems in a more efficient manner.

Total Quality Management (TQM), a management concept developed by

Dr. W. Edwards Deming in the mid 1940's emphasizes that everyone in the organization is a shareholder. This is brought about by Management's involvement and interaction with employees in creating an atmosphere of trust and boosting morale through the education of the workforce.

The exposure to and my buy into the Army's 1960s concept is probably why one TQM guru said to me: "Dave, you don't even know what TQM is but you practice it." I believe that management in the '60s included more one-on-one inter-actions and "common sense." The work environment has changed. Today's hi-tech, hi-speed exchanges seem to be contributing to creating a somewhat faceless work environment.

For what it's worth, on the titular evolution side, in most, if not in all sectors Personnel Officers became Personnel Managers who then became Human Resource Managers. Secretaries became Administrative Assistants who then became Office Management Specialists. And you've probably heard this before: "If it walks like a duck, quacks like a duck and looks like a duck - it is a duck." These people have the same tasks and responsibilities and same scope of work but, new title. Title changes - sounds a little bit like change for the sake of change with no real substance. And for Pete's sake, if you get a new title don't let it go to your head.

Interaction with people and honing your interpersonal skills involves the application of some of the other awareness elements. Like what? Like communicating, listening, and soliciting feedback to name just three. As a reminder, we do not have to reinvent the wheel when it comes to managing people. We all have the tools to become even better and more effective than we are now.

Keep in mind, whether it is managing a bowling alley or a car wash, a mail order company, or an office or a machine shop other people will inevitably become involved. They must be considered in your management equation. You cannot isolate yourself from your environment and people are a part of that environment.

Wouldn't it be nice if the work place was more utopian in nature? A place where everyone could do what they wanted to do, whenever they wanted to do it and without having to consider what anyone else thought? No need to have supervisors. That's not the real world though, is it? Remember – it's an every changing, multi-dimensional, fast-paced work environment.

You, in your quest to become better must work at developing or improving your interpersonal skills. *Interpersonal skills may become even more important to you as you move up the ladder in the organization.* As you move up in the organization your audience may, and in most cases will, change. You may be called upon to deal with a wider variety of people, people from the executive ranks to the "blue collar" ranks.

While with S.J. Groves & Sons in Bolivia I dealt with several vice-presidents and many cabinet ministers and sub-secretaries in the government of

Bolivia. I also dealt with bank executives, hardware store vendors, homeowners, S.J. Grove's employees and their dependents, plumbers and doctors. Plus on any given day I may have been interacting with Bolivians, Germans, Swiss, Americans, Canadians or Brazilians.

On another note, you may even be called upon to mediate disputes, build and lead teams or motivate and persuade others. Scary, huh! Not if you've honed your interpersonal skills to the level that you believe they need to be at. And, you never lose sight of the fact that you are always interacting with someone.

Reality Check: Interpersonal skills, especially when they involve interaction with rank and file employees seem to diminish as one move's up the management ladder. NOT GOOD.

A "TEAM PLAYER", NOT A "YES MAN":

A More Effective Manager is a team player, not a yes man.

The team concept is with us from our earliest days. The family is a team; the church is a team; The Boy Scouts or Girl Scouts are teams; when we make a best friend we in effect form a team. You and your spouse, or companion, are a team.

By definition a team is a group organized to work together. Good so far but in the real world we may not always stay a part of a team. Family members may have disagreements and "split", we may stop going to church or we may become divorced from our spouse. We may change jobs.

In a business environment the team concept goes one step further than the above definition. This concept dictates that whatever the team does it must lead to success; and in the private sector – to profit. If it does not, the risk of failure is increased and the team could be disbanded or, God forbid the business or organization could fail. People may be let go; you may become a free agent again.

What happens if the team is non-productive or does not contribute to the success of the company or organization? On some occasions it may be allowed to stay together and try again; or, several players may be asked to stay together and take on some new players; or, the whole team may be disbanded.

Now that we have further defined the team concept in the work environment, how can you contribute to the team effort? First, let me mention to you how you don't contribute. You don't contribute by sitting in the corner or in the back row with your hands in your pockets playing pocket pool or twiddling your thumbs and saying "Yes sir, I agree" whenever you are asked a question or asked for an opinion. You contribute to the team effort through your interaction with other team members and through participation. Without participation and contribution of the team members, the team concept will never be effective.

It stands to reason then that team players contribute to the group's activities by what's called, "teamwork." Teamwork requires the participation of team members. Teamwork should lead to that sometimes elusive end product that helps make a good management team or organization a great management team or organization: *synergism*; that cooperative action of two or more people, groups or agencies such that the total effect is greater than the sum of the effects taken independently. One head plus one head equals, you got it, not two heads but three heads. Can you have synergism without teamwork? I doubt it.

Your input, no matter how ridiculous or unimportant it seems to you is important. You recognize that while you may not be the team leader, you are still a team member. You have an important role to play in the organization. And, so do your subordinates. Do not expect them, nor encourage them to take everything as the Gospel truth. Encourage their questions and feedback.

Teamwork may mean that team members will have to put their quest for personal gains behind team goals and objectives, at least for the time that they are on the team.

Let's mention team composition. Team members may be drawn from existing company human resources or from outside of the organization. If team members are from different sections, offices or divisions within the organization watch out for "turf" wars. They have to be avoided. If they can't be avoided, they must be acknowledged and dealt with. These could easily arise if team members are vying for the same limited resources.

A good example of this is the team that is put together to recommend to the board of directors the new "right size" of the organization. "Right size," usually means fewer human resources. Right sizing may also have an impact on allocation of funds. Both of which could have a major impact on the operational unit that a team member may manage of supervise.

Carrying the above example a tad further, if staffing levels are reduced for short periods; i.e. seasonal because of employee vacations, an untimely death in an employee's family, an unexpected illness or whatever, what could happen? Grumbling and bitching for sure. But, its times like this that team players relish and rise up to the occasion. Its times like this that separates the "whiners" from the "winners."

Whiners in an organization who bad-mouth people or a section/unit may be insecure with themselves. They are easy to spot and the more effective manager recognizes that employees like this can damage both individual employee and organizational morale. The smarter manager does not necessarily weed out these employees but takes the time to mentor or coach these people in what the team concept is all about. Dealing with a person like this, especially if they have the ear of a more senior ranking person in the organization is another challenge.

Team players who are leaders also recognize that there are teams within the team. I draw this from my participation in team sports. Baseball – the shortstop and second baseman are often referred to as a double play combination – a team within a team. Football – defensive linemen and defensive backs work as a team within their unit and between themselves. How often have we heard an announcer mention a "coverage sack?"

True team players recognize and understand their role on the team. They use, not abuse their role to solicit information or to reach team goals. The classic example of this is the secretary who calls someone and says something along the lines of; "the General or the Director wants to know immediately . . ." Who knows whether this is coming from the General or the Director or from the wannabe secretary?

A notion being touted in some management consultant circles is to create a "Center of Excellence." A Center of Excellence sounds a lot like a well functioning, productive team to me, no?

Bear in mind that you may not be called upon to be a team leader. You may not be in the "loop" all of the time either. Even so, your honest and forthright comments will do more to contribute to the successful completion of the goals and objectives of the team, and organization than just nodding your head up and down and muttering "Yes sir" whenever you are asked for an opinion. But keep in mind and don't get pissed off; your opinion or contribution may not lead to a consensus or majority decision all of the time either.

On a more general note, while it may be difficult for some people to accept, team players usually keep individual possessive pronouns in proper perspective. You rarely hear them say, "My" team or "my" staff or "my" secretary or "my ship or crew." More frequently it's, "our" team or staff or "the" maintenance staff or "the" crew or an even more personal "It was Rosita or Mike who got it done."

A most recent example of teamwork and an acknowledgement from one of its participants happened in the 2008 Olympics. The United States wins the gold medal in basketball. Duane Wade was interviewed after the game. His comment: It's not about the number on the shirt it's about the letters - USA. Now that's a team player.

Reality Check: My gut felling is that there are too many managers out there who gravitate towards being "yes" men. NOT GOOD.

GOAL SETTING:

A More Effective Manager sets realistic goals and objectives for subordinates and for himself.

Don't forget yourself big guy. You are an important player in this. We cannot all be generals, but we can be captains of our own ship. Accomplishment of realistic goals helps us to gain confidence in our subordinates and in ourselves. My goal was to write this book. I thought it was a realistic goal or I would not have set out to do it. My procrastination in getting the damn thing published was another story.

Setting realistic goals and objectives also contributes to maintaining the integrity in any organization. Let me illustrate what I mean by this. In 1973, after the Vietnam War the United States military went to the All Volunteer Force concept. Congress did away with the involuntary draft.

My last military assignment was to the Armed Forces Entrance and Examining Station in Newark, New Jersey. Our mission was threefold: give the mental test and physical examination to all individuals who chose to volunteer to join one of the four services (Army, Navy, Air Force or Marine Corps); after they selected an enlistment option, administer their Oath of Enlistment; and, send them on their way to their service boot camp or basic training center.

Recruiting goals, the number of applicants that the individual recruiter had to recruit and enlist in any given month were so unrealistic for the inner city area that one, or more of the following often resulted: (1) Monthly recruiting objectives were lowered; (2) A substitute person or "Ringer" was used to take either the mental test or physical examination for the real applicant; (3) Mental test score standards were lowered; or (4) Recruiters were relieved and reassigned for not making their quota.

I was giving the Oath of Enlistment to one applicant late one evening, on the last day of the month. The enlistment of this applicant would have meant that the recruiter would have made his quota for the month. However, the applicant did not understand enough English to repeat the Oath of Enlistment after me. Nor could he read the Oath which was written on a large poster behind me.

I denied enlistment to this individual. The recruiter took me aside and offered me fifty dollars to enlist the kid so he could make his quota. I said, "Sarge, keep your fifty bucks and take your wife out to dinner. I know that you're under a lot of pressure but, I can't enlist this kid."

Yet, in retrospect I too was under some pressure. I wanted to maintain some integrity in the system while others were looking for ways to beat the system. Why? -Because recruiters were trying to meet unrealistic goals imposed upon them. Did I report this recruiter to someone for trying to "bribe" me? Not at all! I hope that he and his wife enjoyed their dinner.

Now for the tricky part - *Don't fall into the trap of setting objectives too low.* What you are striving for is to set objectives that are realistic, yet test your abilities as a manager and the abilities of staff to reach these goals.

Sometimes you may have to start with the end in mind and set intermediate goals and objectives to reach that end. The construction of the new USAID office building in Bolivia is a good example of this. End objective; construct a building. Among some of the intermediate goals were: (1) get USAID/ Washington's approval; (2) get funding; (3) find a building site and purchase the property; (4) hire an A&E firm; (5) contract a construction company; and, (6) construct the building.

The construction of this new building started with someone who had a vision, who was creative, who believed that this was needed and who set realistic goals along the way.

These transitional goals and objectives may not always follow a sequential order - be flexible. What if the building site was found and acquisition talks started before getting USAID/Washington's approval? So what? It could have helped convince the folks in Washington to approve the project, especially if the site was inexpensive and better situated to allow for mission accomplishment.

Do you take the risk and spend some time and monies (short of making an unauthorized commitment) on preliminary site identification and testing prior to the approving authority's approval? Depends on how big a risk taker you are.

Once you set your goals and objectives, you'll call upon other awareness elements to help you achieve them. Pieces of the puzzle dealing with prior planning, looking at all of the options before making a decision and taking risks are a few that could come into play as you strive towards your end objective.

Finally, remember that goals and objectives may not be reached all of the time. Why? For one, they may be changed or modified. For another, they may in fact be unattainable.

Aim high, but set realistic goals and objectives. Reaching goals and objectives helps breed success.

Reality Check: I believe that far too often managers who are over-achievers, workaholics or on the fast track tend to set unrealistic team goals and objectives for subordinates. They may even modify or change them along the way to meet their own personal objectives or career goals. NOT GOOD.

FACILITATING AND CONTROLLING THE SITUATION:

A More Effective Manager facilitates and controls the situation.

He takes charge. This is easier said than done.

There may be multiple factors that you have to exert control over; sometimes, all at the same time. This could include control over events, the environment and even yourself.

Example - How about calling and chairing a meeting with some of your customers or your subordinates. Among other things, setting a clear agenda, setting the pace of the meeting, selection of the meeting room and the seating arrangement and setting the temperature in the room allow you to exercise some degree of control over the situation, and the participants.

Control over participants, and subordinates can be a dicey matter. If carried out to the extreme it stifles creativity and leads to, you got it, micromanaging. Let's add another concept to the equation, that of facilitating. To control is to have power over or exercise influence. To facilitate is make easier and to help bring something about.

A facilitator helps bring balance to the event. You can still act as a facilitator at meetings while exercising control. If your objective is to make the meeting easier, facilitate. If your objective is to make the meeting better than the last one, facilitate and control.

The above discussion pertains only to meetings. How do you take charge of a situation when an embarrassing encounter between people happens? A situation when two competing Contractors show up at the same time for a meeting? Sometimes control measures are dictated by the situation.

I just sat down to write this gem when my wife came in and asked me if I had any work to do. She wanted me to go out for a walk with her. Here I was, really motivated to finish this and I replied, "No, not really." I begin thinking to myself; I lost control of the situation. I will wind up going for a walk and freezing my ass off instead of staying by the comfortable fireplace and continuing to write. Hello, I'm back. That's right; I went for a walk and froze my ass off.

Sometimes to control the situation, "Ya gotta know when to say no." I attended a Time Management seminar once. One of the themes was learning how to say "no." Saying "no" does not mean that you are not people oriented or that you are not customer friendly. Learn how to say "no" and how to facilitate and use them as tools to help you bring about whatever it is that you hope to accomplish.

Watch out. Control may have the connotation of power to some folks. Let me a make a few comments about power. Some of you may be in a position that is viewed by some as having "power" – that possession of control, authority, or influence over others according to Mr. Webster. No sweat. Being in a position that is perceived as having power or, in fact having power is common. By perceived power I mean that degree of power that others think that you have. A supervisor or manager does have some control, authority, or influence over what happens in the work environment. Don't fret. What you do with that apparent or actual power is the important factor.

Use of "power" is one thing – abuse of power is another. Even the perception that you are abusing your power/authority/control or whatever else you want to call it will make your managing more difficult.

Don't be afraid of power but, even more important don't let it go to your head. Be prudent in how you use it.

Reality Check: Too many managers still focus on controlling people, rather than managing people or the situation or the event. This leads to micromanaging, stifles individual creativity and oftentimes leads to a misuse of "power." NOT GOOD.

USE OF TIME:

A More Effective Manager makes good use of his time and the time of staff and customers as well.

How often have we said, or heard said, "If only I had more time I would have finished it." More often than not that's an excuse for not making good use of time. Let me rephrase this. Take a look at, and use all of the methods and resources at your disposal to make good use of your time and the time of the employees whom you supervise and other customers as well.

I believe that an important factor, and often times overlooked factor in individual and group time management rests in your ability as a more effective manager to be flexible. Ya gotta go with the flow for yourself and the people whom you manage or provide a service to.

You might want to look at and consider programs such as flex time. How about being really creative and recommending to your boss alternating four-day work weeks with five-day work weeks. He'll probably think that you're sniffing glue, right?

Shift work? I worked for an organization that was paying an inordinate amount of overtime to drivers who were frequently called upon to work on weekends. Solution – Develop a schedule that included a normal Monday to Friday shift and one from Tuesday to Saturday. How was this met by the drivers? Not very good at first but they were professional enough to accept it.

For you, the upbeat side of coming to work earlier than the rest of the staff may be to give yourself extra time to better plan your daily activities. Additional time before the telephone starts to ring off the hook and normal interruptions begin. Arriving earlier may also allow you to avoid early morning traffic jams and gridlocks that caused you to fail the stress test which led to your nickname of "Mr. Grouch."

Making good use of time is, more often than not a personal matter. However, sometimes it can be dictated or influenced by outside events as well.

A more effective manager manages his time wisely. You can do this in the work environment by considering such things as juggling schedules, limiting distractions, not accepting telephone calls between certain hours and realigning work schedules. This all leads to getting the job done in a timely manner. Don't forget, *time is money!* - getting the job done in a timely manner leads to a more cost efficient operation.

Time management in the office will also allow you to put some balance in your life. Here's something to think about from Brian Dyson, CEO of Coca Cola Enterprises:

> *"Imagine life as a game in which you are juggling some five balls in the air. You name them –* **Work, Family, Health, Friends** *and* **Spirit** *and you're keeping all of these in the air. You will soon understand that* **Work** *is a rubber ball. If you drop it, it will bounce back. But the other four balls –* **Family, Health, Friends** *and* **Spirit** *are made of glass. If you drop one of these, they will be irrevocably scuffed, marked, nicked damaged or even shattered."*

Reality Check: Too many managers spend too many days in which they spend 80% of their time on 10% of their issues. And another 10% of their time is spent in a Cover Your Ass (CYA) mode. This leads to those 10 to 12 hour, frustrating work days. NOT GOOD.

IT MAY NOT BE RIGHT, BUT THAT'S THE WAY IT IS - MOST OF THE TIME:

A More Effective Manager may not always agree that something is right but, he should believe that; that's the way it is, at least most of the time.

I am touching the subject of loyalty here. Not blind loyalty, just old fashion employee loyalty to the company and to executives who make decisions that may very well shape employee lives. I am not waving the company flag or saying that company executives, or a supervisor will always make the right decisions.

Some may make a case that there may be a fine line between organizational loyalty and loyalty to an individual within the organization. I am more of an advocate of individual loyalty. The organization did not hire you; someone within the organization hired you.

The organization pays me one might argue. You are correct; but only if you perform satisfactorily in the eyes of a supervisor. Someone once told me that you cannot sue a company; you sue the president of the company of some other official who may be acting in the name of, or on behalf of the company. This is the same idea when addressing loyalty.

Loyalty, or lack thereof in the work environment many times follow a person as he moves on. Probably the most visible example on the negative side can be found in professional sports. Some athletes follow the dream of being on a championship team and winning the coveted ring. After that they follow the big bucks to other teams oftentimes snubbing not only their former teammates but the fans and community that supported them. Having just said what I did, there is nothing wrong with someone wanting financial security. We all do. But the obsession with salary can chip away at the time honored concept of loyalty.

On the positive side loyalty is oftentimes rewarded with promotions; promotions that normally lead to better salaries and possibly to a well deserved "golden parachute" retirement package. Take a close look at your professional and personal goals when assessing this factor in your current work situation.

Let's forget blind loyalty. As I mentioned before you may not always be in the majority, your suggestions may not always be heard, listened to, or accepted and you may not always agree with someone else's decisions. On the other hand, I believe that you should be supportive of those decisions. The unit that you lead should speak with one voice and act as a team.

If you don't agree with something, why should you be supportive of someone else's decisions or a company policy decision? How about resurfacing that team player concept? In some instances you might have a choice. You can ignore the decision, especially one that you think is only a "minor" change in procedure, you can try to reverse the decision or you can accept the decision for what it's worth and carry it out.

What are the ramifications if you ignore a decision? Possible separation, for one - you may get fired. If you try to reverse the decision (Rock the boat?) you can get a certain amount of self-satisfaction knowing that you gave it that old college try but, those clowns in the executive office just wouldn't listen. If you support the decision you may be viewed as a team player. Then again, you may be viewed by your coworkers as not standing up to management, of being a - "yes-man."

An Air Force general was once disciplined and, according to some reports asked to resign because he spoke out against a President's stand on gays in the military. In my opinion, he was asked to resign for the wrong reason. He was sacrificed because he did something politically incorrect. He questioned a decision of the Commander-in-Chief, the president of the United States.

To sit back and accept a decision may not always be, or appear to be in your best interests or, for that matter the company's either. Let your conscience be your guide on this one. Is it worth falling on your sword for? The general thought so.

Should you strongly disagree with someone else's decision, prepare yourself to challenge it and to defend your position. Also, be prepared to pay the consequences.

Stand up and be counted. Voice your opinion. You are not a "yes" person. Be careful, when attempting to evaluate a decision try not to second guess those who may have made it. Why? For one reason or another, they may have had more information than you had to base the decision on. Maybe you were not asked to provide input or you where kept out of the "loop" in the matter. Or it may have come unilaterally from the company CEO or the General or the Ambassador.

Hindsight is easier than foresight. But you still need to remember that, in your mind it may not be right, but that's the way it is - most of the time.

Reality Check: Too many managers are prone to take this concept to the extreme of, "It may not be right but that's the way it is, *all* of the time." Once you do this, you run the risk of becoming complacent and reluctant to challenge, or question decisions. NOT GOOD.

COMMON SENSE:

A more effective manager incorporates common sense into his management activities.

There are probably a lot of scholars out here who are ready to wring my neck and hang me from the nearest lamppost over this one. No need to.

There are many things to be learned in the classroom environment and by attending seminars or by reading your favorite management book or magazine. *In the fast-paced and multi-dimensional work environment however, a more effective manager must be ready, willing and able to face reality.*

All of the formal learning or training that you've received and acquired has to be put to practical use. To me, this is where common sense comes into play.

What is common sense? According to Mr. Webster it is "sound and prudent but often unsophisticated judgment." We all have it. All we have to do is put it to good use.

Become familiar with established company policies and guidelines. Integrate that scholarly learning with your field experiences (sometimes referred to as the school of hard knocks) and the awareness elements mentioned herein. Trust your intuition or "gut feeling" and you have the ingredients that go into this awareness element.

An old colonel once told me that, "Rules and regulations were not made to be broken, but they can be bent." What he really meant was that you, as a more effective manager should always look for ways to get the job done even if it requires bending the rules a bit, and using some common sense. Common sense may, in fact conflict with established company policy.

You may not always have the time, or resources to dot all of the i's or cross all of the t's. What you may have learned in Business Management 101 may have to be bent to fit into a real dynamic management situation. Moreover, whatever you do if common sense tells you that it is time for a change don't be hesitant in your attempt to change the paradigm; or, to change your career.

The following was something that was being sent through the internet. *Forget the political overtones.* Try to read through them and visualize examples in the work environment, rather than in government as mentioned in the obit. Don't be surprised if you find come commonalities as common sense has no boundaries.

"*OBITUARY*

Today we mourn the passing of an old friend, by the name of Common Sense. Common Sense lived a long life but died in the United States from heart failure just after the new millennium. No one really knows how old he was, since his birth records were long ago lost in bureaucratic red tape.

He selflessly devoted his life to service in schools, hospitals, homes, and factories helping folks get jobs done without fanfare and foolishness. For decades, petty rules, silly laws, and frivolous lawsuits held no power over Common Sense. He was credited with cultivating such valued lessons as to know when to come in out of the rain, why the early bird gets the worm and that life isn't always fair.

Common Sense lived by simple, sound financial policies (don't spend more than you earn), reliable parenting strategies (the adults are in charge, not the kids), and it's okay to come in second. A veteran of the Industrial Revolution, the Great Depression, and the Technological Revolution, Common Sense survived cultural and educational trends including body piercing, "whole language," and "new math."

But his health declined when he became infected with the "If-it-only-helps-one-person-it's-worth-it" virus. In recent decades his waning strength proved no match for the ravages of well intentioned but overbearing regulations. He watched in pain as good people became ruled by self-serving lawyers. His health rapidly deteriorated when schools endlessly implemented zero-tolerance policies. Reports of a six-year-old boy charged with sexual harassment for kissing a classmate, a teen suspended for taking a swig of mouthwash after lunch, and a teacher fired for reprimanding an unruly student only worsened his condition. It declined even further when schools had to get parental consent to administer aspirin to a student but could not inform the parent when a female student was pregnant or wanted an abortion.

Common Sense lost his will to live as the Ten Commandments became contraband, churches became businesses, criminals received better treatment than victims, and federal judges stuck their noses in everything from the Boy Scouts to professional sports. Finally, when a woman, too stupid to realize that a steaming cup of coffee was hot, was awarded a huge settlement, Common Sense threw in the towel.

As the end neared, Common Sense drifted in and out of logic but was kept informed of developments regarding questionable regulations such as those for low-flow toilets, rocking chairs, and stepladders.

Common Sense was preceded in death by his parents, Truth and Trust; his wife, Discretion; his daughter, Responsibility; and his son, Reason. He is survived by two stepbrothers: My Rights, and Im a Whiner.

Not many attended his funeral because so few realized he was gone.

Obituary author unknown."

Include common sense in your bag of tools for implementing more effective management.

Reality Check: Too many managers have an inclination to stay within the classroom and look for textbook solutions to problems. They tend to shy away from "common sense" solutions. NOT GOOD.

RESPONDING:

A More Effective Manager responds in a timely manner to everyone.

Rank and file employees need their questions or inquires answered just as much as the boss does. The situation that needs to be avoided is one in which the people whom you supervise will see you as someone who cozies up to the boss - an ass-kisser. The perception is that you drop whatever it is that you are doing to respond to her, while taking days to respond to them. You have to show a sense of urgency to whoever is waiting for your response.

Another undesirable effect of not responding in a timely manner is that a late response to someone's question may result in delays. Not responding in a timely manner could lead to those last minute rush jobs. These not only add stress to the work force but could contribute to poor quality work.

Will last minute responses be needed or rush jobs happen? Of course they will. Nonetheless, as a more intelligent manager you can help keep these to a minimum by influencing events.

One of the events that you can influence directly is response time. "I will look into it and get back to you by noon tomorrow (or later next week)", may in fact be the most appropriate response to a question. This immediate response shows the person who asked the question that you are a good listener, that you are taking an interest in her work and that you are focusing on the issue. See how some of the other management awareness elements begin to complete a management puzzle?

It goes without saying that a correct response given in a timely manner will go a long way in not only setting, but maintaining excellent customer relations. Customer focus comes up in several of these awareness elements. Try to identify your customer. Is he a primary, secondary or tertiary customer? This may help you to establish your response time parameters.

At one of our section staff meetings, in the USAID Mission in Cairo we were discussing customer identification. At that time Cairo was the largest USAID Mission in the world. It had over 100 American employees and over 270 local national staff. The discussion was centered about how many people we actually had to provide support to in the areas of residential and office maintenance. This included office janitorial services and warehousing activities such as moving things in and out of apartments. What did the final count look like?

370	Primary customers; All American and local staff employed by the USG.
210	Secondary customers; Spouses and children of American USG employees who resided in USG provided housing.
100	Tertiary customers; Domestic help working for USG employees living in USG leased housing.

In reality though, for our maintenance and warehouse staff the above mentioned secondary and tertiary customers were in fact their primary customers. Why? These were the people who spent most of the time in the residences. These were the folks that our staff dealt directly with on a daily basis.

The preceding paragraphs dealt with the identification of customer bases. Within each customer base you have to be aware of and identify individual customer needs.

Thinking outside of the box and in a somewhat unconventional way, in my opinion as a supervisor, the people whom you supervise are your primary customers! Why? I go back to the advice that I got from an old colonel and mentioned before – "Dave, if you can't take care of your own people how can you expect them to take care of others?"

Resurfacing response time – again, responding in a timely manner does not mean immediately stopping whatever it is that you are doing. Responding to customer needs goes hand in hand with prioritization of your workload. I may have mentioned it before but if I have, it is worth repeating as the old saying, "the squeaky wheel gets the grease" comes into play - don't get sucked into spending eighty percent or your time on ten percent of your problem customers or whiners. And, that includes co-workers in other sections or organizations and, the people whom you manage.

A more effective manager recognizes where the squeak comes from and responds accordingly. Does it come from someone above him or from someone below him on the organization chart? If multiple squeakers come along at the same time, remember that "first amongst equals" will come into play which in all probability will dictate a response to the person above you.

One final comment about the squeaky wheel; should you become the squeaker (and I hope that you won't) you may not always get results, especially if you continually squeak to those above you. Trust me, the risk is high that you'll be blown off and lose the respect of others. The respect that you worked hard for and earned.

Responding in a timely manner, or just responding at all is getting to be more and more problematic as organizations try to do more with less. Add to this the flood of electronically generated correspondence and you can see why the following article is apropos:

By Mike Musgrove, Washington Post Staff Writer
Friday, May 25, 2007

Last month, venture capitalist Fred Wilson drew a lot of attention on the Internet when he declared a 21st century kind of bankruptcy. In a posting on his blog about technology, Wilson announced he was giving up on responding to all the e-mail piled up in his inbox. "I am so far behind on e-mail that I am declaring bankruptcy," he wrote.

"If you've sent me an e-mail (and you aren't my wife, partner, or colleague), you might want to send it again. I am starting over."

College professors have done the same thing, and a Silicon Valley chief executive followed Wilson's example the next day. Last September, the recording artist Moby sent an e-mail to all the contacts in his inbox announcing that he was taking a break from e-mail for the rest of the year.

The supposed convenience of electronic mail, like so many other innovations of technology, has become too much for some people. Swamped by an unmanageable number of messages -- the volume of e-mail traffic has nearly doubled in the past two years, according to research firm DYS Analytics -- and plagued by annoying spam and viruses, some users are saying "Enough!"

Those declaring bankruptcy are swearing off e-mail entirely or, more commonly, deleting all old messages and starting fresh. E-mail overload gives many workers the sense that their work is never done, said senior analyst David Ferris, whose firm, Ferris Research, said there were 6 trillion business e-mails sent in 2006. "A lot of people like the feeling that they have everything done at the end of the day," he said. "They can't have it anymore."

So some say they're moving back to the telephone as their preferred means of communication. "From here on out I am going back to voice communication as my primary mechanism for interacting with people," wrote Jeff Nolan, chief executive of the business software company Teqlo, in his blog announcing his e-mail boycott.

The term "e-mail bankruptcy" may have been coined as early as 1999 by a Massachusetts Institute of Technology professor who studies the relationship between people and technology. Professor Sherry Turkle said she came up with the concept after researching e-mail and discovering that some people harbor fantasies about escaping their e-mail burden. Turkle, who estimated that she has 2,500 pieces of unread e-mail in her inbox, is one of those people. A book she has been working on for a decade is coming out soon. Turkle joked that it would have taken her half the time to write it "if I didn't have e-mail."

Some people who don't want to go through the drastic-seeming measure of declaring total bankruptcy say they are trying to gently discourage the use of e-mail in their communications in favor of more personal calls or instant messages. "I am reachable, just e-mail is not a good way to do it," said Sean Bonner, chief executive of a news blog network who has automatic responses set up on his work and personal accounts warning he doesn't check e-mail as often as he used to.

Even those who've chosen partial e-mail engagement say they continue to struggle with the question of whether or not to reply. Stanford University technology professor Lawrence Lessig publicly declared e-mail bankruptcy a few years ago after being deluged by thousands of e-mails. "I eventually got to be so far behind that I was either going to spend all my time answering e-mails or I was going to do my job," he said. Thereafter, Lessig's correspondents received e-mail equivalents of Dear John letters: "Dear person who sent me a yet-unanswered e-mail, he wrote, "I apologize, but I am declaring e-mail bankruptcy," he said, adding an apology for his lack of "cyber decency." He eliminated about 90 percent of his e-mail traffic, but said he can't quite abandon it entirely. "The easiest strategy is just to ignore e-mail, but I just can't psychologically do that," Lessig said in an interview.

If there is a downside to completely turning a back on e-mail, it's not one many former users notice. Stanford computer science professor Donald E. Knuth started using e-mail in 1975 and stopped using it 15 years later. Knuth said he prefers to concentrate on writing books rather than be distracted by the steady stream of communication. "I'd get to work and start answering e-mail -- three hours later, I'd say, "Oh, what was I supposed to do today?" Knuth said that he has no regrets. "I have been a happy man since Jan. 1, 1990."

The critics of e-mail themselves have critics, who say copping out is a reactionary and isolationist way of dealing with modern communications. Carnegie Mellon University computer science professor David J. Farber receives piles of e-mail as the administrator of the "Interesting People" technology news mailing list. He has no patience for e-mail bankruptcy. "For a venture capitalist to say something like this -- he should get out of the technology field," Farber said. Wilson, the venture capitalist, did not respond to a phone call placed to his firm -- or to an e-mailed request for comment.

Staff writer Sabrina Valle and staff researcher Richard Drezen contributed to this report.

Reality Check: Most managers make a determined effort to respond to questions and inquiries in a timely manner. GOOD.

BELIEVING THAT YOU CAN DO SOMETHING:

A More Effective Manager believes in himself, in what he can do and in what he does do.

In the work environment this also means believing that whatever a manager does it will make a positive contribution towards helping the organization reach its goals and objectives. The contribution may be viewed in general terms and related to the whole organization or related to the section that he manages. It can also be specific and related to an individual action or to a team goal.

Believing that you can do something may require some extra effort and perseverance on your part to stay focused on whatever it is that you are doing. You may even have to "go out on a limb", take a risk or try to change a paradigm.

As I pointed out earlier, I worked with an executive who had a vision. He believed that it would save the United States Government (USG) millions of dollars if it constructed an office building of its own rather than continue to lease office space at an overseas post. It took him months to convince the folks in Washington that this was the way to go, almost one year to acquire the property, over six months to get the design and construction plans approved and a little over two years to construct the building.

If this individual did not believe that he could bring this project to closure and did not believe that this project was in the best interests of the USG and the government agency overseas and the individual government employee (not to mention a better location to serve the agency's customers), I honestly believe that this project would not have become a reality. And, he did this in two different overseas locations.

I also worked with a very bright, energetic and extremely competent Executive Officer who believed that she could make a positive contribution to the agency in higher level management positions. Her perseverance and networking, coupled with her proven leadership skills and ability to work under duress made this shift possible. Throw in other positive traits such as her interpersonal and negotiating skills and this change became a "no-brainer" to those making assignments. She is now on her way to achieving not only her personal goal but becoming an impact player at the higher echelon levels in the agency wide upper management arena.

Believing, rather than just thinking that you can accomplish something normally leads to a stronger commitment to get it done. Once this sense of commitment is embraced by the team and other players, you'll be that much further ahead in getting the job done. Believe me, it will have a positive, snowball effect on others.

I'll mention a negative. While you may believe in something very strongly, try not to let the conviction become an obsession. Obsessions can often-time cloud good judgment. I have a very good friend who strongly believed that he had to expose what he thought was manipulation of metal prices in the commodities market. The conviction became an obsession. He became flummoxed and exercised some questionable judgment along the way which resulted in loss of job and income, among some other things.

Do not think that you can do something; believe that you can do something.

Reality Check: Believing that you can do something many times involves taking a risk. Because of this many managers, unfortunately only think, rather than believe that they can make a difference. NOT GOOD.

SEXUAL HARASSMENT IN THE WORK ENVIRONMENT:

A More Effective Manager recognizes that sexual harassment has no place in the workplace.

He must become attentive to and sensitive to not only gender issues but age, race or cultural differences; especially those that may fall into the category of discrimination or harassment. This may be a sensitive issue to some but it is, nonetheless a real issue and concern.

When sexual harassment cases surface or get to court, no one wins.

Even the perception that someone might be getting a little pat on the fanny by the water cooler can have an adverse effect on morale. "An adverse effect on morale," you might ask? Damn right! Why? The perception of favoritism will undoubtedly surface. This always has a negative impact on morale.

That leering glance or verbal innuendo may also be insensitive to whomever it was aimed at.

A work-load effect that this awareness element could have on you as a better supervisor is that it may give you an additional tasking; that of *conflict management*. While conflict management could have been mentioned in other awareness elements, or even as a separate topic I mention it here as an over-lapping or cross-cutting concern. As a more effective manager, be on the lookout for areas where conflicts between employees are more apt to happen. Sexual harassment is an obvious area.

On those occasions when love does bloom in the work environment, it is best nurtured in the open and the seed planted in a more romantic environment. What did ex-president Jimmy Carter say that raised some eyebrows and made the tabloids, "I once lusted for a woman." How insensitive that may have sounded to some, but how real to others.

Reality Check: Most organizations and managers make a very good effort in trying to educate employees in this area and more and more managers are becoming more aware of this issue. VERY GOOD.

WORK WINDOWS:

A More Effective Manager establishes and operates within "windows" as much as possible.

He tries to avoid setting finite, end of task deadlines. The "window" referred to here is that time frame that you should allow yourself and staff members to get the job done.

I am not quite sure where to begin the discussion on this one. As a young officer in the military and to a lesser extent later as a manager in the private sector, I too felt, more often than not, "under the gun" to meet deadlines.

The more I thought about this element the more I realized that some of the time I was the one setting the deadlines for myself, and staff. I was the one creating the pressure on all of us. It was me who was saying, "Let's finish this by quitting time." or "Let's finish this by close of business, Friday." What I should have been saying was, "Listen gang, let's complete this within the next three to five work days (or whatever), make sure you plan accordingly and we'll meet and discuss our progress in a couple of days."

Will all deadlines disappear with this approach? - Probably not. Why? For one, a last minute project or reply will inevitably come up or be required. For another, something might interfere with your plan or work timetable. You may have to focus on something else for the next day or two. You may not always have the luxury to work within "windows."

Incidentally, when you are working on a project and have the chance, examine the project and see if it can be completed in phases. If so, that's even better. Give yourself a window to complete phase one, phase two, etcetera. Phases then become a series of windows to operate from. The point is, if you have the opportunity to plan work completion within windows, do it.

You will see that certain types of work or situations better lend themselves to this approach.

In one location I was at we were very careful about making sure that we did not disrupt the work force when doing minor construction work when reconfiguring office space. We decided to go with four hours overtime after normal work hours. Night one, dismantle walls; night two, install aluminum framing for new walls; night three, put up gypsum/wallboard and prep for painting; night four, paint.

Everyone was happy. No one had to put up with noise or dust pollution or the strong smell of thinner or paint. And, a few blue collar low income maintenance workers got some overtime. In this example Saturday was ruled out. A long three day weekend was coming up and the evening work allowed the workers to also enjoy the long weekend with their families.

You may be in a business where work windows will be dictated by special conditions. The Kaffen Company was involved in industrial maintenance. A good deal of the work had to be done when there were few people around or when a plant was shut down. It was not uncommon to work on Saturdays, Sundays and holidays or from 11:00 p.m. to 8:00 a.m.

You will find that working within windows will also make the task or project more readily acceptable to the work force. Those of you with the attitude of, "I work better under pressure" will soon find out that you work even better under less pressure. Give it a chance.

Time management and workload distribution also come into play here. Bring in a sense of prioritizing and you have other awareness elements working together to complete a management puzzle.

Reality Check: I still see too many last minute rush jobs and back-breaking deadlines being set. Unrealistic deadlines tend to burn out employees. In the long run creativity and productivity will inevitably suffer. NOT GOOD.

BRAINSTORMING:

A More Effective Manager practices the art of brainstorming.

Believe it or not, we do this sub-consciously almost on a daily basis. To some, brainstorming is a little like shootin' the breeze or throwin' the bull, except brainstorming normally should focus on a single event or issue or project. It may even provide some input that will make decision making or problem solving less complicated.

By definition a "brainstorm" is a sudden clever idea, and brainstorming is the shared problem solving in which all members of a group spontaneously contribute ideas. Shared problem solving means just that. You share your ideas or thoughts with your brainstorming group. Let it all hang out in these sessions - Creative thinking?

No matter at what level of management that you are at, if you call the session, the selection of the people you want to participate in it is essential. Don't forget that old geezer in the corner. Should you bring in an outsider, someone not employed by the company? Why not? Depending on the situation, maybe one or two of your customers would fit very nicely into the group.

The physical location that you select to have a brainstorming session in should be kept free of outside distractions. Have your secretary hold all telephone calls (even those from the president). And, if you are a real risk taker – don't accept calls from your spouse.

Also, try to identify what your purpose is and what you want to get out of the session. No matter what, facilitate and control the situation, not the participants, but don't let them wander too far from the topic either. Your goal should be to do this without stifling creativity or putting a damper on the session.

Depending on the composition of the group, you may want to incorporate a bit of role playing here. Assuming another identity may push your creative thinking to a new level.

Free thought leads to a more successful operation. Think independently – act as a team.

Brainstorming and teamwork could result in synergism and a larger "Center of Excellence." Again, see how the various pieces that a more effective manager should be aware of fit together to complete the puzzle?

Brainstorm my friends, it really works.

Reality Check: Most managers do a good job at using brainstorming sessions. GOOD.

THE WHAT IF SYNDROME:

A More Effective Manager does not dwell on the word "if."

Why? To me, more often than not the connotation of "if" is that we are not satisfied with what we did or the way things turned out. "What if I had done it differently?" "What if I had just waited a little longer?" "What if I had listened a little more attentively?" "What if only they had given it a chance?" "What if the dog didn't stop to take a pee? - he would have caught the rabbit."

What was done was done for God's sake. Ninety percent of the time you won't be able to change the results anyway. But, let's turn this into a positive. A learning experience if you will.

The 1st Brigade, 101st Airborne Division (Screaming Eagles) came up with a "Lessons Learned" publication after almost every combat field exercise that they completed when they operated in Vietnam. It was a short critique of their performance. It was along the lines of, "If we did this, the results would have been this" kind of thing. Included were both the positive lessons learned and the negative lessons learned. Remember positive and negative feedback in a previous awareness element?

I am not suggesting that you run your office or shop like a military organization. I am advocating that you take the time to evaluate performance, not only individual performance but operational performance as well (more on this in another awareness element).

Remember the old saying, "First time, shame on you second time, shame on me." "What ifs" should lead to performance evaluations that will help you prevent making the same mistake twice. Learn from the "What If" syndrome.

Avoid using the "What If" argument as a negative, scare tactic to say "No." "If" we let one person do it, *everyone* will want to do it. Ridiculous! "If" we let someone get away with it, *everyone* will try to get away with it. Ridiculous! "If" we issue a foot massager to one employee, everyone will want one – Ooops! - Maybe not a good example.

The one I like best is, "If" we do it, it will set a precedent. Setting a precedent can have a positive effect on an organization. And, if in fact the precedent becomes the new rule, maybe the old rule needed to be changed.

"If" the North Koreans were to nuke Seoul tomorrow it would have a profound effect on the world community. What is the risk of that happening? Probably as great as the risk of setting a precedent that will have a detrimental effect in the work environment.

Reality Check: Some managers tend to overplay the "What if" argument; sometimes to the extent of calling attention to their individual need to control not only a situation, but people as well. NOT GOOD.

EVALUATING:

A More Effective Manager evaluates.

He evaluates the performance of the individuals he manages. He also evaluates his own performance and the overall performance of the organizational unit (team) that he may manage or supervise.

I have said a mouthful here right? It is not as complicated or difficult as it seems. There are three distinct categories involved. First there is employee/subordinate evaluation; remember, the workforce is composed of people. They may make mistakes. The U.S. Army philosophy of individual performance evaluation based on the "Whole Man" concept is just as valid today as it was in the 1960's.

Be reminded that someone's weakness may be someone else's strength, and vice versa. If your company does not have some kind of employee performance evaluation appraisal system, develop one yourself, at least for key staff members.

However, don't forget that there is a lot of subjectivity in rating individual performance. You have to be objective. Most important, you have to be fair. Put that one "dumb thing" that Joe did six months ago behind him if you believe that it is the fair thing to do.

Second there is your own performance; remember too that you are, "people." Some folks may think that you're a jackass or a horses' ass, but we all know that you're not. You're just as human as the rest of the team and you make mistakes to. Do not be too hard on yourself, big guy. As the manager, you are the one in the spotlight or under the microscope. Your head will roll if a major screw up happens because you are not going to "pass the buck" or fix the blame. But, when evaluating your individual performance be as objective as you can and be fair to yourself as well.

Third there is team performance; remember, the team is comprised of, you guessed it, people. Be as objective and as fair as you can in evaluating the team's performance, just as you were in evaluating individual performance and your own performance. You may not have put the team together. Regardless, it is you who provides the leadership to the organizational unit or team or individuals whom you manage.

I have found out over the years that the most objective performance evaluations are the ones based on *continuous assessment*. The better managers are always looking for ways to improve performance. To improve performance, you must be able to evaluate performance. You do this by continually assessing how you and others are performing as individuals and as team members.

Are you meeting individual or team goals and objectives? To what degree are goals and objectives being met? Are you achieving results? Are your customers satisfied? If they were satisfied six months ago, are they still satisfied today?

Performance ratings based on results evaluation rather than employee technical skills or effort, may be a major consideration in the evaluation process in many cases. How about considering some balance amongst these?

Let me jump back to evaluation of subordinates for a moment. The Army Officer Evaluation Report form had three sections for the rater to complete: one was space for a short narrative; one was a scaled, 1 – 5 rating of such things as physical fitness, decisiveness, communications skills, etcetera (I think that there were 12 areas); and, one was a graph to rank the rated individual with others that the rater evaluated.

A colonel rating me once gave me a less than the highest score in the physical fitness block and I had just "maxed" the annual Army Physical Training (PT) test. I asked him, "Why?" He told me that no one was perfect.

He believed that of all the categories in this section a lower rating for physical fitness would have the least amount of negative influence on others who were looking at the report in the bigger scheme of evaluating, within the centralized promotion system. While he gave me the highest scores in all of the other areas, he believed that he was fair in doing what he did. He also gave me an option. He told me that if I selected any other area for a lower score, he would give me the highest score for physical fitness.

The military rating system, at least when I was in the service had one rater. The concept of one rater was based on the premise that if the officer doing the rating did not know what the rated individual was doing, or how he was doing it, he should not be his rater.

To make the system transparent and as a matter of a "check and balance", each report also had a section for a reviewing officer (endorser) to complete. This was normally the rater of the officer doing the rating. This was help for both the rater and the person being rated. You can't do it alone. Neither can you be the sole person to input data that will, in some cases have a profound impact on the career of the rated individual.

Why? Your writing skills may suck for one. If you are in an organization that centralizes promotions, some people may focus on narrative rather than looking at the whole report. And even worse, focus more on the last report.

While it was not mandatory for the rater to solicit comments or feedback from others, everyone that I knew, as a matter of common sense, solicited feedback. This was formal or informal over a cup of coffee or a drink at the Officer's Club or at a party or wherever. People talked to one another. This sounded pretty basic to me.

As a matter of precaution, when you solicit feedback or input, be careful and professional enough to weed out misinformation. Know your source of information. There may be a back-stabber or two within the organization.

Here is another personal example coming up. I was up for promotion from Captain to Major, after Vietnam which was in a period referred to as a "Reduction in Force" (In the private sector this was later called downsizing and even later, rightsizing).

Result at the first go around – fully qualified but not promoted. I wasn't quite sure what this meant so I went to see the military folks in the Pentagon.

The Major whom I met called my attention to the fact that on the very *first* evaluation report that I received as a member of Adjutant Generals Corps, and written by a Captain one comment in the narrative said that "this officer performs all assigned duties with little or no supervision." "Little supervision" was his focus.

I pulled out and showed him a damn near "max" (actually it may have been a max) evaluation report that I received about four years later. To go along with the superlatives noted by my rater, included in this report was the endorser comment. "Captain Korponai is the best, [not one of the best mind you, but the best] young Adjutant Generals Corp officer that I have seen in my career. This came from a full colonel who was on the Brigadier General's list. He had over twenty years of service.

While the colonel's statement did not swing the centralized promotion panel in my favor, the point is that the endorsement, at least to me gave transparency to the reporting system at the grass-roots level. It brought a little more fairness into a system. What this myopic knucklehead at the Pentagon failed to do, in my opinion was to focus on the "whole man" concept.

If your company has a rating system and you are a rater, don't try to shirk away from this responsibility by circumventing it or by "passing the buck." I was with an organization once that had a system in place; albeit, it was a cumbersome system that required an inordinate amount of time from many supervisors and employees to administer.

One way to abuse, rather than use this system is to call someone in whom the rater could influence and maybe even have some control over. Call them in under the guise of evaluating the operation when in fact they are there to evaluate the employee that you, operating within the system guidelines were supposed to be evaluating. You pressured and received "negative" input from the person you brought it - you got someone to do your dirty work – to provide you with that one negative "impartial" statement that could be used to skew the report to a lower rating.

What's more, if you were really on the fast track and didn't have the time, or patience to mentor the person whom you were supposed to rate, who really cared? You in effect have washed your hands of this task also.

The above example is not intended to fix blame. It is intended to surface a potential shortcoming in evaluation systems. In the real world, many employees are critical of evaluation systems, whatever the reasons may be. You as a more effective manager must stay within the existing parameters of the system, or try to change it to make it fairer.

If you can't change it, then what you must do is: *use it, not abuse it.*

Collectively, performance evaluations, especially individual evaluations tend not to fit the normal Bell shaped distribution curve. On the one hand they are often times inflated; on the other, biased. The solution to bring more fairness into any evaluation system is a joint responsibility. It starts with you, the more effective manager to keep the rating process professional, not personal. It continues upward to those who monitor the process. They may be in a position to identify prejudicial rater trends. If they do so, they must have the professional courage to confront those who abuse, rather than use the system.

Reality Check: I truly believe that most supervisors recognize that no one, including themselves walks on water. Most of them try to make evaluation systems, no matter how cumbersome they are, work. GOOD.

STAYING CALM, COOL AND COLLECTED:

A More Effective Manager stays calm, cool and collected and keeps himself under control.

Wow, is this one is easier said than done. This can really test your mettle. Holding back an impulsive or spontaneous reaction to stimuli that you find distasteful or unprofessional can be extremely difficult. A young male in heat thinks with his small head, not with the one on his shoulders. A more effective manager must think with the head on his shoulders at all times.

The most difficult situation for most people is the one where a verbal, negative remark is directed at them in front of, or loud enough for colleagues, peers or subordinates to hear. Whether it is made in the office, shop or at a company social function, your first reaction to strangle the son of a bitch (SOB) who made the remark is expected, and may be justified.

I once had a colleague come into my office when I was in charge of a General Services operation that included the custodial program. He told me in a loud voice and in an obnoxious manner that neither the janitors, nor I were doing our jobs.

He told me that his immediate and surrounding work area was a "pig sty." My reply to him in a voice not quite as loud or offensive as his was, "Let's go down to your office and identify the little piggy's who are spilling coffee and dropping crumbs on the carpets and floors, leaving half-eaten sandwiches and dirty dishes on their desks, tables, or the photocopier and missing the wastepaper basket when they attempt to toss away their trash while sitting at their desk."

To some, this response may appear to be one of "fixing the blame" and not the problem. Not to me. Why? I knew the customer for one. The problem I identified was one of an overworked and super tired employee venting, for whatever reason on an issue that was easy to pick on. The real issue was not with my job performance or the overall performance of the custodial staff. Lesson learned? You bet – Individuals need to be reminded of *shared responsibilities*; in this case, the need to pick up after themselves. An admin notice was sent out to everyone reminding them of this.

My above response was made somewhat easier by two factors: one, I knew the customer; and two, I was in his area the day before as part of my "Management by Walking Around." It was clean as a whistle. This guy didn't have a leg to stand on. By the way, we never did go down to his area, nor did I hear from him again regarding my performance, or the quality of the custodial services.

Written memorandums or letters that are based on rumor or hearsay and not on facts are another form of annoyance. I received one such piece of correspondence that made a not to subtle accusation that I had made an unauthorized commitment on behalf of the United States Government. This had to do with a residential lease. The individual alleged that I had made a verbal commitment to lease a house and that we had started making renovations prior to signing a lease agreement.

This was totally incorrect. The fact was that no work was done on the house by USG employees until nearly two weeks after signing the lease contract. The work he questioned was being done by the owner as part of her renovation plan in preparation of putting the house on the market.

My first reaction was to strangle the idiot who wrote the memo. My second reaction was to go to my boss or bypass him and go right to the top. My third reaction was to write a reply to my accuser stating the facts. This prevailed. Written accusations give you time to analyze the situation and to make an even more rational decision as to what your response will be.

E-mail adds a new dimension to this. It is just too damn easy to include everyone and his brother on the Cc line. The concerned individual/complainer/whiner or whomever can easily lose sight of - solving problems at the lowest level possible. They often-times add folks who are two or three rungs above them on the management ladder. Why? Who knows?

Some of you may have picked up on a customer service theme that implies that; "The customer is always right." This is far from the truth. More on this in a later discussion about making folks happy and meeting their expectations.

How do you respond to or educate or inform an irate customer who just might happen to be wrong? In a calm, cool, and collected manner I hope.

Develop and incorporate into your work day things that will contribute to helping you remain calm, cool and collected and negate that urge to bang your head against the wall. A few to consider may be ten to twenty minutes of meditation or a brisk walk around the block (or parking lot if the block it too long).

Good karma according to the Dalai Lama includes spending some time alone every day.

Stay calm, cool, and collected. Keep in mind that the person who angers you controls you!

On a final note, in the fast paced, ever changing work environment it is not uncommon for one to become frustrated or stressed out. We are all exposed to stressful situations. It is how you handle these times that really counts. I have been living and working overseas for over 35 years. I use the "F" word a lot. Not the "F" word that some you are thinking of – in my case its' Foreign. I am a Foreign service officer, I live in a Foreign country, I work in a Foreign country, I eat in Foreign restaurants, I rely on Foreign customer services and utilities; I am in a Foreign country because I chose to be in a Foreign country, no one twisted my arm.

I may not have hot water, or any water for days at a time, the electricity may go off at any time, the static on the phone line during international calls may sound like a bowl full of Rice Crispies – but to get back to reality – my way of dealing with this is to look in the mirror and say to myself – "Self; you're here on your own free will." Then I think about the service members serving in places like Iraqi and Afghanistan who are not there on their own free will.

Sometimes a good way to deal with stress is to stop feeling sorry for yourself. You're a more effective manager and a leader, remember?

Reality Check: Most managers show a willingness to restrain themselves quite nicely. GOOD.

A GOOF DAY AND INNER PEACE:

A More Effective Manager knows when to take a goof day off from work; a day to chill out.

You feel it. It may have started the day before. You went against the grain and trusted your memory and you forgot your four o'clock appointment with a new client who was thinking of buying one hundred thousand dollars worth of your company's products.

You finally got a date with "Ms. Right." You wined and dined her until one o'clock in the morning to the tune of several hundreds of dollars. When you dropped her off you got a "Good Night" peck on the forehead and an, "I'll think about it" when you asked her for another date.

When you got back to your apartment you set the alarm for five a.m. instead of seven a.m. You got up on the wrong side of the bed and stepped in a pile of dog crap on the way to the bathroom. Your biorhythms are all in synch, on the low side; and, your stars are so far out of line that when you call Alice Astrologer's hot line, you keep getting a wrong number.

Something tells you it just ain't gonna be your day! Take a goof day, a mental health day, a chill-out day, a venting day or whatever you want to call it. Why? Your peace of mind is important. Maybe the goof day is just to lounge around all day with your spouse or companion. Take it. You earned it and deserve it.

This is part of the bigger picture referred to in some circles as *stress management.* Stress leads to distress. As a more effective manager you have to stay focused. You need peace of mind. The previous awareness element of staying calm, cool and collected also helps in your stress management. Once again we see how some of these awareness elements complement one another to make you a better and more effective manager.

Disengage; not only on a goof day, but when you take your vacation. The office will be there when you get back. It's not going anywhere. Have trust and confidence in your subordinates that they can continue to operate in your absence.

Indulge yourself in a passion that fuels your deepest inside calm – painting, reading, swimming with the dolphins or whales, walking in the mountains, love making or whatever. Believe me; it will lower your stress level. It'll also put a smile on your face and, that will go a long way with those who associate with you. *Get to your level of inner peace.*

When away from the office, how do you stop worrying about the person who is after your job or the dreaded back-stabber; the person who talks behind your back when you're not around? These may be valid and real concerns. What goes around comes around and hopefully you, as a more effective manager will have created a work environment that put a damper on this kind of employee behavior.

The risk of being let go while being away from your job is minuscule. Having just said that, there are still a few senior managers out there who lack professionalism or morale courage to look someone in the eye and let them know that their services or employment are no longer needed. The pink slip or other notification may indeed come when you're in Florida, or wherever. If that becomes a reality, as the bumper stickers used to read in Colorado; Shit Happens!

A lot of managers simply do not disengage when they leave the office to go on vacation. Why? Sometimes it's because of their worry about the concerns mentioned above; sometimes it's because they are workaholics; and, sometimes it's because they just love their job!

Try to remember what someone said - Making a living is not the same thing as making a life.

Reality Check: A greater number of managers need to chill out a bit more in the work place. NOT GOOD.

NICE GOING!:

A More Effective Manager rewards people in the work environment.

Rewards range from the simple pat on the back to the note that says, "Nice Work" to the verbal, "Great Job," to the letters of commendation or appreciation, to the wall plaque and the ten year service pin. The incentive cash award or product stipend may also be appropriate. The group recognition for winning the shop bowling league may be a Saturday afternoon Bar-B-Q. The rose to Helen on Mother's Day is a form of recognition.

The Armed Forces Entrance and Examining Station (AFEES) I was assigned to in beautiful downtown Newark, New Jersey was one of four large AFEES on the east coast. If I remember correctly, the other three were located in Boston, New York and Philadelphia.

As the Processing Officer it was my responsibility to co-ordinate all of the activities in the station. First came the administering of the mental test then the physical examination, and, after the recruiter "sold" the enlistment option, the swearing in of the recruit. Final administrative processing was booking transportation for the new recruit to the appropriate service boot camp or basic training center.

After being there about six months and implementing and incorporating some changes we started receiving the large AFEES of the Quarter award, every quarter. The commander of the station said, "Dave, great job, but I can't keep giving you a Joint Service Commendation Medal every three months for your efforts." Since my military career was on the downward slope on the road to oblivion, I told the colonel that just his telling me that was reward enough for me. The most under used reward is the simple "Thank you for trying."

An ambassador at one overseas Post that I worked at had an "Employee Appreciation Day." He closed down the embassy at high noon one day each year and encouraged all employees, and their families to go to a popular, out-door, lake-side picnic area not far from town. Free bus transportation was provided. It was not mandatory to attend. If you didn't go, you could still take the half day off.

Don't forget to include the little guys in your equation. When I was in Bolivia running the fifty-five person General Services Office (GSO) I started a GSO Employee of the Month award. I brought the Administrative Assistant into my office and told him that this was primarily for the maintenance, warehouse and janitorial staff and drivers. We designed and printed up a nice certificate. We also made a display board where the person's name was engraved on a plaque which made for permanent recognition. We also had various people from within the organization make the presentation. The person who made the first presentation was the Mission Director. This set a nice tone for this monthly event.

The three most important areas that keep employees satisfied, happy, and dedicated to the organization are: job stability (with career development); recognition (rewards and training); and, compensation (salary). Develop a program or set of criteria that works for you and your organization in rewarding people.

Don't forget to reward your outside customers or clients. Can you offer them a discount or a "two-for-one?" How about sending them a two line note that says; "Thank you for being our customer. What can we do to better serve you"?

Along these same lines, I had just been hired by the USAID to manage the GSO mentioned above. I was on the job for a month or so and decided to give the staff members a half-day off on their birthday. This went on for about three or four months before the front office got wind of it and I got a call from my boss. His question - Was what I was doing in accordance with USAID or American Embassy policy? I told him that I didn't know. I also mentioned that it was my policy and either USAID or the Embassy could adopt it if they wanted to - Not the right answer! Needless to say I had to immediately cease this practice. However, my stock went up with the rank and file and down a tad with some of the other executives who thought that this should have at least been an embassy wide policy since it would effect the whole work force. As you can imagine, the adoption of this as a Post policy was not forthcoming - Win some, lose some.

I have been in organizations that have over utilized rewards/awards and I have been in organizations that have under utilized them. Put on your thinking cap, be creative, brainstorm, but in any case reward people.

Reality Check: We can all do better in this area, especially in the use of the no cost sayings like "Thanks" or "Great effort." NOT GOOD.

THAT "HALF-STEP" TO THE REAR:

A More Effective Manager knows when to take that half-step to the rear.

Taking a half-step to the rear in this sense does not mean backing away from something or retreating. It is not a sign that you made a mistake. It is not a sign that you change directions or have a difficult time making decisions.

This half-step to the rear gives you the time to re-evaluate, to reassess or to pause and reflect on whatever it is that you have done or are about to do. It will give you an opportunity to see the bigger picture more clearly. I word to the wise though; don't use this as a crutch to second guess yourself.

Taking that half-step also indicates patience; patience with yourself and with anyone else who is involved; be they your customers or co-workers. That's right, I said with yourself. You are an important part in this equation. You've got to have patience with yourself. Call it self-discipline.

Patience involves developing an understanding that it may take time to produce a desired result. The pace of getting things done may not always be the one that you would like to see. It is essential to remember that while the pace may be too slow for you, it may be too fast for others.

Taking a "half-step" to the rear to reevaluate/reassess/reflect on what is going on in front of you and all around you is important. If you are still in the planning phase, in the long run you may even gain some time to develop modifications or whatnot; and time is the wisest counselor of all.

How about taking a second look at a current policy? This is the same idea. Take a half step to the rear, take off the corporate blinders and look at the big picture impact and ask yourself questions. One key question is: Why are we doing it this way?

And for those of you in the service sector or contracting out for a service, is the cheapest service the best business practice in the long run? Maybe not; especially if it is not done in a timely or professional manner. Or worst yet, you are asked to do it over for a second time.

Reality Check: Too many managers still fail to realize that; that that half-step to the rear may lead to a longer and more productive step forward. NOT GOOD.

ROOM FOR IMPROVEMENT?:

A More Effective Manager knows that there is always room for improvement in what he does, subordinates do or the organization does.

This was probably one of the easiest awareness areas to identify.

A more effective manager always looks for ways to make improvements in what he and subordinates do or in what the organization does. Why? Because improvements usually mean that things will get better. Maybe even easier!

Speaking of getting better, remember that this is the real world that we are managing in so I'll throw in a negative. Sometimes things can't get better. Why? Resources may have dried up - You may not have the human or capital resources available to make something better.

So what do you do if this happens? Maintain. Maintain the status quo. Keep doing things at the level that you have done them and maintain the quality of services or products that you are currently providing. Keep your customers happy and content. Then when you do get the resources, make those changes that will improve whatever it is that you want to make better. The important thing is not to regress or let things slip. Have patience, stay calm, cool and collected and keep "trying" to make things better with what you have to work with while still educating your customers and not burning out your staff or yourself.

This is probably a good time to think ahead and to plan for the future.

My last assignment with USAID placed me in an environment where I was wearing three hats: Executive Office for USAID, Management Officer for the Department of State (DOS) and manager of a service provider that was quasi-independent of USAID or DOS management. During the last year of so of my assignment we were involved with the major tasks of transforming a consulate into a full-fledged embassy which included recruiting additional staff and renovating/expanding over-crowed facilities, finding an adequate residence for an ambassador in a small and tight housing market and consolidating and regionalizing services mandated by Washington bureaucrats sitting thousands of miles away who knew, what appeared to be in most cases very little about how to operate in the local overseas environment that we were in.

What was one of my goals through all of this as a manager? Maintain services and some semblance of order and preserve tranquility for myself and the staff that I supervised.

By recognizing that the learning process never stops, a more effective manger now takes what he has learned and makes those constructive, tangible improvements that will have a positive effect on the way that things are done. This should lead to increased employee productivity. Throw in the positive effect on the intangibles like one's morale and attitude and you have a more healthy work environment.

To make improvements, you may have to "reengineer." Reengineering normally refers to overhauling (changing) how the organization or operational unit does whatever it is that it does. It may involve focusing on goals and objectives that too often are determined not by customers but by some centralized planning committee sitting hundreds or thousands of miles away from the implementers. Kind of like the old Soviet style, centralized management systems. And we all know how that wound up.

I said; "focusing on goals and objectives." Use management by objectives as one of your tools to help you look for things that may need improving. If needed, modify objectives along the way as the situation changes or dictates. You may get a call from your Controller cutting monies from your budget; something like this will undoubtedly mean some modifications to how things are being done.

What about the reengineering of a component of the organization - the component that you manage. Why not? If you come up with reengineering ideas for your office or shop, share them with your supervisor. Strengthening organizational components normally contributes to the establishment of a stronger and more efficient operation or organization. Don't' get sucked into the trap of believing that re-engineering means reducing staff. It does not.

Unforeseen problems may lead to improvements, especially if you are flexible and creative. Suppose your goal is to produce 400,000 widgets per quarter this next calendar year. Two months into the year a major power failure shuts the plant down for one week, six months into the year a transportation strike results in non delivery of materials needed to make the widgets and nine months into the year the widget machine breaks down. Quarterly production objectives are not being met.

Problem? - Maybe yes, maybe no. If you change delivery schedules with some of your customers: maybe not. Double or triple shifting may be in order. Take that half-step to the rear, brainstorm and keep your customers in the loop and you've got things under control once again. Good job Charlie.

Think outside of the box. Evaluating the situation mentioned above may lead not only to improvements, but even to significant changes in the way that the company will do business. For example, the company may consider purchasing its' own fleet of trucks to pick up materials and deliver end products. A full time mechanic may be hired to perform scheduled preventative maintenance on vehicles and/or equipment.

Speaking of thinking outside of the box, the most creative people, as a group that I have come across were those involved with on the ground, in the air or on the water direct military combat operations. When people's lives are on the line, you'd be surprised how creative one can become. Doctors, paramedics, police officers, firemen and those involved in life threatening situations aren't too far behind.

As was mentioned earlier, you don't have to wait for things to become broken or run amok before trying to enhance them. Use whatever skills and tools that you have to look for ways to make improvements and constructive change.

Making improvements in the work environment will make your managing less complicated. It will give you more time to focus on other things. Improvements may even lead to more leisure time for you and the folks you manage.

There is always room for improvement.

Reality Check: It is much easier to identify what needs improvement than it is to get changes approved and implemented. NOT GOOD.

UNDERESTIMATING YOURSELF:

A More Effective Manager never underestimates himself or his capabilities.

It's true, you can go for it. Once you have your goal set, or your plan organized and in order, and you believe that you can reach it or do it it's time to execute your plan. It's time for action. Take the education that you have and the experience that you have gained and put them to work. So what if you only have a high school GED and four years of experience.

Whether it is a personal or work-related goal that you want to reach, it is imperative that you do not underestimate your ability to reach it. If you want something bad enough, you will get it. If you want to implement something that you have worked hard on, you will. Maybe it is going for that associate degree at night. Getting one may enhance your marketability in the future if you wind up looking for a new job.

I know someone, very well in fact who had the opportunity to go to college right out of high school. He chose instead to get married and start a family and go to work at age twenty-one; So far, so good. Some people are content and happy to do this and no more.

This kid was not; he wanted more. At age twenty-three he decided that there was more in life for him than just raising a family and delivering pizzas. He decided he wanted a college education after all. His schedule looked something like this:

8:00 A.M. to 4:30 P.M.	Full time job, five days a week
5:00 P.M. to 6:30 P.M.	Study, at least five days a week
7:00 P.M. to 10:00 P.M.	Classes, three nights a week
4:00 A.M. to 6:00 A.M.	Second job delivering over two hundred newspapers, seven days a week
6:30 A.M. to 7:30 A.M.	Study, at least five days a week

What were the results? Deans' list, a deep appreciation that there are a heck of a lot of opportunities in life and raised self-esteem knowing that through hard work and a desire to improve himself (in this case, through education) he'd have a better chance to accomplish whatever else that he may choose to do in the future.

The main point is that he did not underestimate himself or his capabilities. He reached the realistic goal that he set for himself. More power to him. I am not using this as an example because this person is one of my sons. I mention it because if you look around you you'll see something like this unfolding a hundred times over. Join the club.

Maybe he comes from a family of late bloomers. I didn't get my MBM until I was fifty-three years old. My wife, an accomplished artist didn't start painting again until she was in her mid-fifties.

The point is; it is a lot easier to quit on yourself by looking for excuses based on, "Well, I probably could not have done it anyway" than it is to face yourself in the mirror and say, "I have the capabilities to get what I want through perseverance and hard work. I may have to sacrifice some, but, I'll go for it." Throw in a little bit of luck and, who knows what might happen.

As a better manager you can't let a negative attitude of underestimating yourself carry over into the work environment. Remember, subordinates are looking to you for direction. Your supervisor is looking to you to give that direction to whomever you supervise. If you underestimate yourself and do neither, you are only asking for trouble.

Lastly, how about that promotion you turned down because you realized that it not only meant more money, but it meant more responsibility as well, and you thought that you were not ready to cope with that yet. Hogwash! A more effective manager is an achiever; maybe not an over-achiever but, an achiever never-the-less.

Whether your life changed because you rocked the boat and got fired or pissed off your boss or got divorced or had a bad personal relationship with someone, try to keep a positive attitude. There is something out there for you, probably better than what you had before. Go for it, and ...

Never underestimate yourself.

Reality Check: The majority of managers that I know realize that there is nothing wrong with not being on a fast track. They do a good job at working up to their potential. GOOD.

GIVING YOURSELF CREDIT:

A More Effective Manager gives credit where credit is due, and that includes to himself.

Don't be reluctant to pat yourself on the back. You're not bragging or boasting. You worked long and arduous hours and you busted your back to get something done. You planned, you organized, you made a decision, you implemented and you followed through. You took a risk. You played an important role in this and you earned the respect of your coworkers. You can justifiably take some credit for a job well done.

This is not going against the "We, not me" principle or team concept. Why should you be aware of something like this to be a more effective manager? I believe that this adds to your self-confidence, self-esteem if you will. It balances. Six months ago you took the heat for something that did not go too well. You did not pass the buck. Now you have a chance to congratulate yourself for a job well done. Treat yourself to an extra thick steak or that double martini or that long lunch.

If you're lucky enough to be in an organization that has some kind of rating evaluation scheme and you are asked by your rater or supervisor to provide some "bullet" items as to what you accomplished during the past year, do it. Better yet, if he asks you to write your own evaluation report, do it.

I felt at one time that when my rater, a Lieutenant Colonel asked me to write my own evaluation report it was because he really did not know, or was not interested in what I was doing. Not so. This was his way of rewarding me. His way of saying, "Thank you for doing a great job." This could be your supervisor's way of giving you a chance to "blow your own horn." Go for it if given the chance.

Don't be embarrassed by displaying those items that you really worked hard for and are proud of. That college diploma, those certificates and those special letters of thanks will not only look good on your desk or wall, but they will give your office or work area that personal touch. They will also serve as a reminder to you that you are an achiever, a go getter, a doer. Give yourself credit.

This is a good opportunity to take care of yourself. Remember that you are Numero Uno – Number One! Again, this is not going against the team concept. It is not being selfish or self-centered. Why? If you can't take care of yourself physically, mentally, emotionally or financially – how can you take care of subordinates in the work place?

Reality Check: As a rule most managers don't give themselves enough credit for the hard work that they do. NOT GOOD.

"I DON'T KNOW":

A More Effective Manager is not afraid to say, "I Don't Know."

Let's face it, no one knows it all. And that includes you. Besides, who wants the reputation for being known as a "know it all?" There is linkage here to the other awareness elements related to responding, learning and questioning.

A key point to take from this is that if you do not know the answer to a question, you will have to learn where to find it. In doing so, you may even find some secondary information that you can store and use at a later date. It's always best to let the questioner know that you'll find the answer and respond to his question in a timely manner. See how you've turned this "negative" into a "positive" learning experience?

Remember the old sayings, "Only the nose knows" and "Ya can't bullshit a bull-shitter!" Plus, it is downright embarrassing to give out wrong or misinformation to customers, to subordinates, or, for shame, to your boss. If confronted with a question that you don't have an answer to, stay calm, cool and collected and most important, do not be afraid to say, "I don't know."

Reality Check: Far too many managers have a tendency to say "No" rather than to say "I don't know" - the answer to which may, in fact lead to a "Yes." NOT GOOD.

THE SIX P'S:

A More Effective Manager plans ahead and remembers the six P's; Prior Planning Prevents Piss Poor Performance.

This sounds so basic that it is almost embarrassing to mention. Right! Wrong! Develop a routine that allows you to be constantly aware of this. I cannot emphasize enough how important this element is to a more effective manager.

Outside of the box for a minute - A brief note on planning your personal affairs - The Six P's concept is not only an important factor in managing in the work environment. It is an important factor in managing yourself and your personal affairs. You heard me, now listen to what I said: "It is important in managing yourself and your personal affairs." Don't get frustrated. I am not talking about planning for or managing those things that you have no control over. Like your ex-spouse. Or your ex-lover who is now on the verge of filing that palimony suit if you don't send her your left testicle in a jar within the next fifteen days. I mention this here lest you let personal problems carry over into the work environment; problems that can be attributed to lack of planning in your personal life.

Back to the work environment - The Six P's pertain to those factors that you have some control or influence over. The posters in the United States Army, in the early 1960's all read, "Plan Ahead"; same idea. What does planning entail? (Let's presume that you have already established your goal or objective).

Planning is basically trying to think of all the areas that may have an impact on, or influence over your reaching your goal or objective; then, developing an orderly program or scheme to achieve the desired result, end or objective. It is also time to start defining team and individual roles, tasks and responsibilities.

Prior planning is preparation. To prepare is to work out the details of and to make ready beforehand whatever it is that you are working on. An example at grass-roots level follows. A friend of mine, a graduate in languages from Providence College took over his father's successful painting and wall-papering business. I decided to paint the interior of our house and asked his advice. Simple he said, "Prepare the walls and ceilings and slap a coat of paint on them." However, he told me that the "prep" works of sanding, spackling, masking, etcetera would take 80-90 % of my time. Slapping on one or two coats of paint was the easy part.

Planning also takes discipline.

The pieces linked to this could include those awareness elements related to soliciting feedback, focusing on the issue or the problem, anticipating, making good use of time and brainstorming. See how the components that you should be aware of as a more effective manager fall into place in the planning phase of whatever it is that you are planning for?

Once more remember that these elements are the components that will assist you to complete the planning puzzle and contribute to your becoming a more effective manager. Depending on the complexity of the plan, some of the elements mentioned in the preceding paragraph may or may not be applicable. However, they are there to be used as management tools if needed in your planning phase.

Keep in mind that planning is one thing, implementing and executing the plan is something else. A key, basic ingredient to remember here is to do first things first! Don't jump the gun. Don't get itchy feet. Have patience. Sound familiar?

Doing first things first will allow the implementation of the plan to proceed with fewer problems. That's right, "fewer" problems. I have yet to see a plan executed that did not have a few glitches in it. Don't panic. Your well thought out, prior planning scheme will prevent a poor performance by those called upon to implement the plan.

Planning also requires taking a look at the big picture. But, don't go overboard and stifle individual creativity. *Remember, wars are won with planning. Battles and skirmishes (implementation) are won with individual courage and initiative, flexibility and teamwork.*

Don't forget the acronym KISS; Keep It Simple Sweetheart. The more complicated things get, the easier it is for things to go wrong. Remember the six P's, KISS it and do first things first.

Example of prior planning; some companies have a 3-5 year marketing plan. That's prior planning. When you establish a vacation schedule for employees whom you supervise; that's also prior planning.

On a much larger scale, I was told that Adolf Hitler had the map makers in Germany delete the village of Wildflecken from maps published in the mid or late 1930's. He established a secret SS training base there complete with overhead camouflage for the whole compound and parts of the village itself. German maps that fell into the hands of allied soldiers gave no clue as to the existence of a village, let alone a training base. That's ultimate prior planning.

Reality Check: Most managers make an honest effort to plan ahead. GOOD.

STRENGTHS AND WEAKNESSES:

A More Effective Manager recognizes and acknowledges that everyone has strengths and weaknesses, including himself.

Being honest with ones' self is the important thing to remember here. Self-criticism should lead to self-evaluation.

Some of my weaknesses, at least in my own mind are speaking in front of large groups, over-simplifying and my literal interpretation of things. I am not very comfortable when I have to stand up in front of people to make a presentation. It may take me a day or two to prepare myself for this chore. I am not too excited about responding to questions spontaneously or off-the-cuff either. I could easily wind up shooting myself in the foot or putting my foot in my mouth.

Why did it take you three weeks to get up the courage to ask Harry Heartthrob or Ms Right out for lunch or for a date? A little shy, perhaps? Palms get a little sweaty before that important meeting with the executive committee? What do you do about those butterflies in your stomach before an interview?

If we truly reflected upon and gave some attention to our weaknesses, and took the time to really analyze them, then we might be able to get something positive out of this. In my case I take some extra time in the preparation of a presentation. I try to anticipate the questions that will be asked and have some prepared responses ready for them.

For some people acknowledgement of their weaknesses, even to themselves is very difficult. This is the first hurdle to get over. This may be especially difficult for those of you with the Macho Man/Narcissus complex. Lighten up on yourself. Relax. I am talking about taking an honest look at yourself. A little bit of self analysis and recognition of one's strengths and weaknesses never hurt anyone. Try it. Take a look at yourself in the mirror and get to know yourself. I believe that the following anonymous lines put the exclamation point on this very nicely:

The Man In The Glass

"When you get what you want in your struggle for self and the world makes you king for a day,
just go to a mirror and look at yourself and see what that man has to say.
For it isn't your father or mother or wife whose judgment upon you must pass;
the fellow whose verdict counts most in your life is the one staring back from the glass.
Some people may think you a straight shooting chum and call you a wonderful guy; but the man in the glass says you're only a bum if you can't look him straight in the eye.
He's the fellow to please, never mind all the rest, for he's with you clear to the end; and you've passed your most dangerous, difficult test if the man in the glass is your friend.
You may fool the whole world down the pathway of years, and get pats on the back as you pass; but your final reward will be heartaches and tears, if you cheated the man in the glass.

And for those of you who are sports fans let me put it to you in this way. This is all about a concept that says; Play within yourself. Throw in a little bit of luck and things begin to fall into place. Example of a gridiron experience - You bet. My senior year in high school I played in a state football all-star game with a kid who made "All-State." He decided to go to a large mid-western power house and ended up holding blocking dummies for four years. I wind up at the University of Connecticut, which at that time was not an Eastern power-house, captain the UConn team in my senior year and some forty years later still hold some school records.

Be honest with yourself. Recognize and acknowledge your strengths and weaknesses.

Finally, you may recall the old farmer's advise – The biggest trouble maker you'll probably ever have to deal with, watches you from the mirror every mornin'.

Reality Check: Some managers find it difficult to admit to their own weaknesses. NOT GOOD.

BEING CONSISTENT:

A More Effective Manager is consistent in what he does.

I touched on this in the discussion of the evaluation of performance. There is a heck of a lot more to this than just consistency in the way that you evaluate people or performance. There is consistency in the way you treat all people.

There is consistency in your work habits. These do not go unnoticed by co-workers, by the way.

There is consistency in the way you interpret company policy. Is it consistent with the way other managers in the company interpret them? This is important if you manage in a company with offices or plants in different locations and deserves special comment here.

There is a certain amount of subjectivity that goes into policy interpretation. Consequently, there may be differences or inconsistencies in interpretation. If you believe that the policy is not being interpreted correctly or consistently throughout the company, maybe it is time to rock the boat a little.

I am familiar with an international agency that did not interpret a contracting policy consistently throughout the agency. This policy pertained to salary contract negotiations for new employees. Some contracting officers were focusing primarily on a person's prior salary history. If a person's salary history fell below the advertised position grade, the new employee was brought in at a grade and subsequent salary at least one grade below what was advertised.

Some hiring officials were focusing on the "whole man" concept. They were considering prior salary history, education level, prior work experience and other general qualifications, like language ability. Someone rocked the boat and a bulletin was circulated that helped clarify the policy in question.

The clarification favored the latter interpretation. While salary history was a consideration, the overriding factor was the candidate's overall qualifications. A fully qualified individual was not penalized because he happened to come from a work environment that may have paid obnoxiously low wages. Now there is consistency in the interpretation of this policy agency wide. A fair system became even fairer.

Reality Check: Unfortunately, still too many managers let prejudice and bias and personal goals obstruct their consistency in the area of managing human resources. NOT GOOD.

THE MEANS MAY NOT ALWAYS JUSTIFY THE END:

A More Effective Manager understands that the means (methods) may not always justify the end (result) that he hopes to accomplish.

This is another sensitive area since results may be the only yardstick by which performance is measured. What this could lead to however is an attitude of "Screw it, them or whatever – just get me results."

While there are cross-cutting aspects of other elements here, I thought this item worthy of separate attention. Why? Because once you become an even more effective manager you'll see that it is not that difficult to get people to do what you would like them to do, and in the way that you would like them to do it. In other words, you can still get results without "Screwing it, them or whatever."

Let me illustrate. The United States Government (USG) has a "smokeless work environment" policy that was put into effect some years ago. In effect, this banned smoking in all USG owned or leased buildings, excluding residences. However, no implementing guidance was received from Washington as to what to do with offenders; so far so good - no micromanagement.

What was published at one Post was a "Three strikes and you're out" policy. The policy made it required for a coworker to report a smoking violation in the work place to their supervisor (strike one on the offender). The second offense required the offender to participate in a smoking cessation program (strike two). The third offense required the offender's supervisor to place a written counseling note in the offender's personnel file that "may affect future step/grade increases and the employability of the offender." (Strike three). And, maybe you're out for good. Hasta luego amigo.

Orwell, in his novel *1984* predicted Big Brother's (governments') encroachment on individual freedoms. Fidel Castro, through neighborhood committees "rewards" people for "informing" on their neighbors. Is that next in the work environment mentioned above - a promotion for the employee who reported the smoker?

While some may argue that nothing was being encroached upon since the employee was not "free" to smoke in the work place, to me the "three strikes and you're out" policy had shades of Orwellian and Castronian implications. The threat of being fired, although not required for the third offense implied that the policy makers in this organization, while acting as if to care for an employee could have fallen into the trap of overlooking their qualifications, or future potential as an employee. Having just said all this, I do not know of anyone being fired because of getting caught smoking in a no-smoking area.

Let me carry this example one step closer to the absurd. Since it is "required" policy that a co-worker reports a smoking violation, what happens to the co-worker who knows a violation occurred and did not report the violation? Does he also get a reprimand for not complying with policy? In my opinion, in this case the means (three strikes and you're out policy) does not justify the end (a smokeless work environment). And believe it or not, I say all this as a person who has never smoked.

I once heard someone say that, *"It's not where you start – it's where you finish."* You can still get to the finish line without intimidating folks or being a horse's ass.

The means may not justify the end.

Reality Check: Sometimes a strong belief that the ends may justify the means leads to mismanaging of human resources and micromanaging. NOT GOOD.

JUMPING TO CONCLUSIONS:

A More Effective Manager does not jump to conclusions.

This could pop up when you have to make an assessment, or evaluation of something or someone. It could also become a factor when you have to make an "on the spot" decision.

A better manager gathers as much information as she can and evaluates that information before making her final choice. As previously mentioned, if you are in a position that requires interpretation of a regulation or policy statement it is even more important that you have all the facts in front of you. Avoid reading between the lines or stop reading at mid-sentence or midway through a para-graph. A more effective manager must be as objective as possible. You can't be pre-judgmental and look for only the answer that you want to hear.

If you are in a position that involves the interpretation of policy that pertains to a personnel matter, including recruitment, retention or dismissal, remember that you are dealing with your company's most precious resource; people. *My rule of thumb here has always been to lean toward an interpretation that favors the recruit or employee.* Why? One reason is because I'm a "people oriented" person. Another reason is that in the long run, the least amount of employee turn-over the better it is for you and the company.

Also, not jumping to conclusions will enhance your image as a manager who is not only fair, but one who does look at all of the options before making a decision. Not jumping to conclusions, along with looking at all of the options before making a decision gives you an opportunity to apply the 360 degree assessment concept. It will give you time to look into your crystal-ball to try to determine the long-range implications of your decision.

How will the decision affect those people who may be in front of you, as well as those on either side of you or behind you? How will the decision affect your company's image in the community or in the industry? Whether or not you are approaching the limit of your work time-frame "window," or your deadline, be careful and avoid jumping to conclusions.

Reality Check: Most managers do a pretty good job at not jumping to conclusions. GOOD.

MAKING EVERYONE HAPPY, ALL OF THE TIME:

A More Effective Manager understands that she cannot make everyone happy all of the time.

She can be as accommodating as possible, but no matter how hard she may try, someone will complain or bitch about something. People in the Army tried to put this in a humorous light by saying that, "If you weren't bitchin', you weren't happy."

Abraham Lincoln is often credited with saying:

> *"You can fool some of the people all of the time and all of the people some of time, but you can't fool all of the people all of the time."*

I like to paraphrase this to say that:

> *"You can make some of your customers happy all of the time, and all of your customers happy some of the time, but you can't make all of your customers happy all of the time."*

I say this because there are some folks out there whom you won't make happy no matter how hard you try. Let's face it, some people can live in a palace and still bitch about the plumbing. I may have mentioned it already but it's worth repeating; there are "squeaky wheels" and whiners out there.

When interacting with a customer on an issue that may have a direct effect on him that he may perceive as being negative, bring him into the loop when you think the timing is right. Explain the rational behind your decision and hope for the best.

You may find it difficult to say "no." But, you will find that most people are very understanding when they are kept informed of what is going on and what is happening. We can't always get our own way. In those instances when you anticipate a problem with someone, you may want to bring your supervisor into the loop first and get his or her input and, hopefully support.

The bottom line is to treat people with respect and in a reasonable and fair manner. Above all, have patience, be a good listener and stay calm, cool and collected. You've read this someplace before, right?

Look at the flow. An *informed* customer is normally a *satisfied* customer. A satisfied customer is normally a *happy* customer.

Let's expand on the theme "The customer is always right" mentioned earlier on.

I have been in customer service related positions for over thirty years. I still want to regurgitate my breakfast, lunch and dinner every time I hear someone say that "The customer is always right." The knucklehead who coined this phrase should be sequestered in a locked room with an over-flowing toilet for a fortnight.

On the contrary my friends, *"The customer is not always right."* Customers may think that they are always right, but in the real world that we manage in, this just isn't so. Try not to let yourself or any members of the team that you managed get lulled into believing this concept. Customers are, you got it, people, and people are sometimes wide of the mark.

Alas, the customer may not always be right, but he is - still your customer. You can't just write him off.

Reality Check: Most managers understand the importance of customer service. (GOOD) Regrettably, too many still get cornered into catering to the "squeaky wheel." NOT GOOD.

LOOKING BACK:

A More Effective Manager looks to the past as a learning tool.

Satchel Paige was one of the first and most famous of the black American baseball players. One of his most famous quotes was "Don't look back - something might be gaining on you." But he was one hellava a pitcher who did learn from his past experiences in baseball.

While this is a cross-cutting theme with several other pieces of the puzzle it is worth a brief, separate comment.

You can't bring back the past but you can learn from it. Draw on your past experiences. Don't be afraid to say things like; "When I was in ... we did it this way" or "I remember when ..." This is the retention part of the learning process, the process that never stops. A word of caution, unless you learn something from past experiences and apply it to the present, looking back may only impede creativity and progress.

When I was in Cairo, and we were upgrading our warehouse to accommodate more customer storage I recalled an incident in Bolivia where we had three warehouses with platform, balcony type storage space about twelve to fifteen feet above the ground floor. None of the platforms had railings. Decision: install safety railings. Decision made in May 1991. Railings finally installed in Warehouse #1 in February 1992. Warehouse #2 and #3 still did not have safety railings as of July 1993. Why? What's the hurry, no one had fallen off in the past - you guessed it - twenty years! Thank God there was no OSHA in Bolivia. If all went well, railings would have been installed in both Warehouse #2 and #3 by the end of calendar year 1993.

You better believe that the new balcony storage areas constructed in Cairo had railings.

A saying on the internet I recently saw said: "Yesterday was history, tomorrow is the future today is a gift – that's why it is called the 'present'." We can all learn from yesterday, do what we have to do today and plan for tomorrow.

Reality Check: Sorry to say, but, a hellava lot of good managers still cling to how things were done in the past. NOT GOOD.

PASSING THE BUCK:

A More Effective Manager does not pass the buck.

I believe that it was President Harry Truman who once said, "If you can't stand the heat, get out of the kitchen." I think he also said, "The buck stops here." Notwithstanding the fact that the first time I was eligible to vote, I voted for Barry Goldwater "Give 'em Hell Harry" made some good points.

What is "Passing the Buck?" - Passing the buck in this context means looking for a scapegoat, trying to pass the blame.

Sean Connery starred in the movie, **Rising Sun** a mystery involving business espionage and a Japanese hi-tech company. One scene has Connery, a detective Captain with the San Francisco Police Department mentoring a young, fellow detective. The dialogue of Connery went something like this:

> *"The Japanese have a saying, "Fix the problem, not the blame. Find out what's f_ _ _ _'d up and fix it, and then nobody gets the blame. We're always after who f_ _ _ _'d up. Their way's better."*

This was an unforgettable scene that could fit into a host of fast-paced, multi-faceted work environments. Why? Part of the reason is that there are still too many folks in management positions who focus on a fast track career rather than on the future of others in the organization. They prefer to fix the blame rather than see their career tarnished by a questionable decision that they may have made.

If your work environment still revolves around fixing the blame rather than the problem, you've got to make every effort to change it. Change the paradigm. I have participated in far too many meetings, and still do where professional executives, in my opinion still have this myopic mindset. Comments, typically center around; "Well, I didn't approve that. Who did?" or "Someone must have misinterpreted what I meant. I'll find out who." or "Let's find out who did that dastardly deed."

Don't misunderstand me here, we should all be held accountable for our own actions and be prepared to shoulder the blame for our own mistakes. As a more effective manager you may have to take the heat for a subordinate's mistake. What? - take the blame for something you did not do? Not all of the time, but, why not?

This is not covering up for a subordinate's or co-worker's mistake. There may have been a breakdown in communications. You may have assumed that whatever it was that was done was done correctly. You may have contributed to the mistake. You've fixed the blame, squarely on yourself.

If you are into the concept of empowering your subordinates to make decisions, this is even more important to understand. Support for subordinates takes on many different forms.

In a previous awareness element we touched on delegation of authority but not responsibility. This still stands. However, there is the issue of *shared responsibility*. That needs some amplification. The concept that all employees are shareholders in the organization not only implies, but means shared responsibility. It also means that a supervisor cannot wash his hands of his responsibility as a leader.

Don't pass the buck.

Reality Check: Sadly to say, too many senior managers, especially those who micro-manage tend to ask "Who?" before asking "Why?" Why? - Who knows! NOT GOOD.

ASSUMPTIONS:

A More Effective Manager does not assume anything.

Why? - Because assuming something will undoubtedly make an *ASS* of *U* and *ME*.

Take this one for what it's worth. Common sense tells us that because of a manager's workload, he may have to assume some things. I assume that Suzy Secretary will make my appointment. What if she fails to make your appointment with Mr. Slick, the Senior Vice-President from the New York firm that was interested in investing some capital in the company that you work for? I assume that Suzy will finish the report. What happens if it did not get finished?

We are only touching the tip of the iceberg here and mentioning only assumptions of things to be done. How about the assumption that if something was done, it was done correctly? No need to ask questions or to follow-up, right?

This is a very subjective matter and a difficult element to discuss in concrete terms or with concrete examples. As you try to flatten out the organizational unit that you manage by delegating more authority, or empowering those whom you supervise you may tend to make assumptions more than you did in the past.

Delegation of authority, but not responsibility pops up in several awareness elements. You, as the more effective manager are responsible for what the unit you supervise does, or does not do.

Remember that delegating authority and empowering employees not only implies, but demands that trust be inserted into the equation. Trust in subordinates that you have because you took the time to mentor and you took the time to develop the person whom you are delegating or empowering to. You've now got peace of mind.

Reality Check: Most managers balance assumption with hard evidence and fact fairly well. (GOOD) What some do, too often is assume that they can do someone else's job better than the incumbent can. NOT GOOD.

GO FOR IT:

A More Effective Manager plans then implements decisions in a timely and decisive manner. He goes for it!

By decisive I mean go for it with the determination and gusto to see that whatever it is that you are doing, is carried out to its' fullest. Let it all hang out. Be firm, yet aggressive in implementing. There is nothing to hold you back now that it is time to execute your plan or the company's plan.

Hard work went into getting things this far along. Believe it or not implementing or executing a plan, especially one that you played a key role in developing will give you a better sensation than that first date with Harry Heartthrob or Ms. Right or your first orgasm (maybe that's stretching the point – but you get the picture). It is exhilarating to see the seeds of your labor come to bear fruit. But, don't get too carried away yet partner.

Implement in a controlled manner. Take it one step at a time – do first things first. Bring some of the other awareness elements into the picture.

Continue to evaluate feedback. What are you learning from this? The learning process never stops, remember? Anticipate reactions. Keep evaluating. Be flexible. Stay calm, cool and collected, especially if it seems like there are a few more glitches to iron out than you anticipated.

Implement in a timely manner. Don't procrastinate any longer. Why wait? A lot of time had gone into the planning phase. You have mapped out a plan for success. But, hold on. Depending on what it is that you are going to implement, timing may be important. Try not to confuse procrastinating with waiting for the right time to implement.

Several years ago, while in Bolivia I was flying back to La Paz from Cochabamba. Cochabamba is the principal coca growing region in Bolivia. One of the programs to help reduce the growing of this hardy, high-value cash crop involved "crop substitution." A fellow sitting next to me was a hi-tech agricultural specialist who specialized in satellite image interpretation. Basically, he analyzed color satellite photos to determine soil consistency/composition. He then went on to recommend what crops would be best suited to grow in this area.

This guy was smart and thorough. His report not only included the findings based on his satellite image interpretations. It also included the findings of several previous, on the ground studies as well. One study was done almost twenty-five years earlier. You probably guessed it by now. His findings were almost identical to the ground study that was done twenty-five years earlier.

If the agency that had commissioned the study twenty-five years earlier had implemented a crop substitution program based on these findings, maybe Bolivia would not now be the second largest grower of the coca plant in the world. We learn from the IF syndrome, right?

When the decision has been made to implement a plan and a time has been set to implement it, go for it. Implement in a decisive and timely manner.

Reality Check: Most managers show willingness to implement in a timely and decisive manner. GOOD.

NETWORKING:

A More Effective Manager networks.

Within the organization this should include people who may be above him, below him or on either side of him on the company organization chart. Some will certainly be colleagues outside of the work environment in other similar of related businesses, groups or organizations or wherever.

Networking is a 360 degree activity. In the old days it was referred to as developing contacts or just keeping in touch. This is the same thing here.

Why 360 degrees? For one, you never know who will give you an inspiration or suggestion that will help make your managing less difficult. Keep in mind who is number one, numero uno: it's you. Joe Smuck, the clown in distribution, may marry the boss's daughter and wind up as a senior vice president. And he was on the shop bowling team with you, you lucky bastard. Granted, you can't network with everyone. Give it your best shot though.

In today's hi-tech arena, tools such as electronic mail allow you to more easily keep up those personal and business friendships that you develop when attending conferences or seminars. These, in my opinion should supplement but not replace the old standard - the business card. Pass them around.

And don't overlook the networking that you can do through membership in local activities such as the Chamber of Commerce, the Lion's Club or the Masonic Lodge if you happened to get invited to join. Volunteering in community service activities, such as the Girl Scouts of America or the YMCA are also good places to make contacts. If you are a sportsman, joining a local softball team or playing in a recreational basketball league or in pick-up games may be in order.

How about keeping in touch through the "old boys" network? There is nothing wrong with that. How about keeping in touch through the "young ladies" network? There is nothing wrong with that either. In reality we now have two parallel and, at times competing systems. Great! The end result should bring more gender balance into the workforce, especially at executive levels.

The bad rap on the "old boys" system was that it kept too many old farts around. These were the guys who had lost sight of the concept of the need for change and who where content with the status quo. They were often-times viewed as "yes" men rather than free thinkers and innovators.

One man who wasn't a yes man was a WWII veteran who, I was told was recalled to active duty to serve as the G4 (Logistics) of the 1st Brigade, 101st Airborne Division in Vietnam in the mid-1960s. While he didn't ask for this assignment he was asked to come back on board by his "old cronies" who had served with him. His reputation and expertise as a logistician was un-paralleled. His ability to coordinate logistics for this highly mobile Brigade in a fast-paced, combat environment was credited with saving many lives.

Networking can help simplify your day-to-day management as well. How? Networking allows you to tap into other sources of information - information that you may be able to put to good use in your organization. You can learn from others through networking.

One final thought on networking. It can assist you in career development. Actually, this was some advice that I received from a rather senior Major in the Army; advice that I only heard and didn't listen to I might add. His advice - If someone you have befriended is on the fast track grab on to his coattails, and enjoy the ride as he takes you along with him. There is nothing wrong with that.

And, don't forget luck and timing as you network. They may not only turn out to be factors in your becoming a more effective manager, but they may play a role in your career advancement as well.

Reality Check: Most managers network well. GOOD.

ATTITUDE:

A More Effective Manager has a positive attitude.

This is sometimes difficult to do. It is tough to be the eternal optimist. Sometimes the glass is half empty. The road may not always be paved and smooth but you can't turn back the odometer as someone once said.

Let's start from the beginning. If you get down on yourself, don't stay disheartened or depressed too long. If you get down on someone else, don't hold the grudge too long. You can't afford it. Why? In the first place, it's not very healthy for you. In the second place, it probably won't help matters anyway.

Whatever happens, don't carry a negative attitude into the workplace. You can prevent this carry-over by being cognizant, through your situational awareness and knowledge of where you are, and who you are. Believe it or not, being aware of the situation that you are in will help you focus on attitude.

A positive attitude will help turn negatives into positives.

We have just gotten started on this one. How about turning that negative or embarrassing situation into a positive? What do you say to Harry Heartthrob when you accidentally spill a glass of port on his lap while imbibing a nip or two at his private club after playing two sets of tennis? And he's wearing white tennis shorts? "Gee Harry; let me help you out of those things?"

Or what do you say to Ms Right when you spill a glass of port on her lap. And she's wearing a two hundred dollar white mini-skirt that shows legs that should be insured for one million dollars? "Red is very becoming on you!"

How about that feeling that you're walking on a treadmill? You never seem to get ahead. You take eighteen hundred steps forward and you feel that you're still in the same place. You didn't accomplish a freakin' thing. Everything seems to be in a constant work-in-progress mode. It could be time for an attitude check right?

Plus, a positive attitude will aid you to become happier with yourself. Someone mentioned that the happiest people don't have the best of everything they just make the best of everything that they have. For the more effective manager, this includes making the best of what, and who you have to work with in the environment that you manage in.

Start with a positive. Remember the old saying; "*Yes*, we have no bananas today." (Thank you Samia)!

Take a look at some of the vocabulary that you use in the workplace. Did you have a "terrible" day at the office? - Probably not. It may have been a trying day but not a terrible day. It would have been a terrible day if your tie got stuck in the shredder.

You just got back from a two hour, three martini lunch and your boss is standing by your door with his hands on his hips and a scowl on his face. Oh boy, did you make a "bad" decision? - Probably not. It may have been a questionable decision, but not a bad decision - it would have been a bad decision if you didn't come back at all.

Look for ways to give yourself an edge when it comes to developing and maintaining a positive attitude. Attitude carries over both ways; personal to work and work to personal. Whatever it takes, keep a positive attitude to assist you to turn crisis into success.

A positive attitude will keep you a "winner" and not turn you into a "whiner." Speaking of which, a more effective manager recognizes the importance of being a graceful winner. No need to gloat over successes: but, as mentioned already don't forget to give yourself credit either.

A positive attitude is contagious. No matter what happens or how bad it seems today, life does go on, and it will be better tomorrow.

When the chips are down most of the more effective managers who I know seem to reach inside for that extra bit of, "who knows what" to pull them through. A large part of that has to do with having a positive attitude.

Reality Check: I believe that most managers have a pretty good attitude in the workplace. GOOD.

DOING WHAT YA GOTTA DO:

A More Effective Manger does what he has to do.

And, if at all possible this starts with him being where he wants to be and doing what he wants to do. My first exposure to this was in my freshman year in college. Our freshman football coach was a *Harvard* graduate who shared time with the Kennedy's and went on to serve with the U.S. Department of State. At UConn – football coach and physical education teacher. Why? He was doing what he wanted to do. When he was not selected as the new head varsity football coach it brought tears to the eyes of many.

You have to be content with yourself because some of the things ya gotta do in the work environment may not always be popular. How about telling your colleague, who's your next door neighbor that he has been laid off? Or due to budget cuts you have to inform employees that ten percent of staff will be laid off for an indefinite period or let go permanently in the "near future" as part of the company's right-sizing exercise.

Managers are not always nice guys. I once accepted an employee for a lateral transfer into a position that I had direct supervision over. It took me less than one week to realize that this person was not the right person for the job. It was uncomfortable for both of us.

However, in all fairness to the employee, for a second time we sat down together and went over her scope of work and tasks and duties and what was expected of her. Although this was not an entry-level position and the employee had been with the organization for fifteen years or so, we nevertheless established a short probationary period. At the end of this period and after discussing her performance with her and with my supervisor, it was decided that it was in the best interests of the organization, and the employee to move her back into her old position. She gracefully accepted this and, in my opinion she felt relieved to get back into her familiar routine where she performed in an excellent manner.

Depending on the conditions in your office or shop, you may have to rock the boat a little to get someone's attention. You may have to walk out of a meeting that you find unproductive. You may tick somebody off – even your supervisor. Doing what ya gotta do may not help in your career development either.

How about that career change? I was between jobs from late April, 1989 to early November, 1989. An opportunity came up for me to work with that small, but highly successful industrial maintenance company in Connecticut, the Kaffen Company. I left Bolivia and high-tailed it to Connecticut.

In retrospect it wasn't a bad decision. In addition to honing my management skills and learning more about myself, I kept the creditors off our backs by paying the bills while my wife built a smaller, but very comfortable house in La Paz. The separation was not welcomed. It was no fun being a geographic bachelor for fourteen months.

Speaking of opportunity, *a more effective manager is always on the lookout for windows of opportunity* in the work environment. These opportunities might help solve or resolve problems. Problems from utilization of human resources to implementation of a policy change. They may come up at any time and they may not last too long either.

Example - Trying to accelerate the hiring of an individual who will fill a critical, one of a kind position in your shop. The Director of Human Resources is going on a three week vacation in two days and everything comes to a standstill when she's gone. Your window of opportunity to intercede and to try to bring this hiring action to closure isn't very big.

Miss it and the potential employee may find another job. Worst, the hiring process may have to start all over again.

Reality Check: Too many mangers are more content with sitting back and going with the flow of the status quo rather than, doin' what they gotta do. Because of this, too many opportunities go by the wayside. NOT GOOD.

STROKIN':

A More Effective Manager may not always tell it like it is.

On the other hand, he doesn't fabricate stories or perjure himself either. Sounds contradictory right? It's not. This goes hand in hand with knowing your customers.

At times you may have to stretch the truth a tad when dealing with people. When Terri Typist or Mike Messenger come in looking like they've been run over by a bulldozer the night before, tell them they look good, not great, just good. They will appreciate your sympathy, and good judgment.

When Bob or Betty Boss come in looking like they went twelve rounds with Mike Tyson the night before, tell them they look like hell. They will appreciate your candidness. Get the picture? *Ya gotta learn how to stroke folks.*

Some of you are probably thinking that the examples above should have been reversed. Maybe this is so. Use your own judgment and some common sense in how you want to stroke the people with whom you have to deal with and relate to.

How about the appointment that you were late for because you trusted your memory rather than keeping your mobile phone turned on? When you remembered it you where lining up that twenty foot putt on the ninth green. What do you tell your client – you were out gathering additional information?

Strokin' may also involve some public relations (PR). Let me illustrate this with the following example. In the mid 1980's the governments of the United States and Bolivia tried to get the Bolivian growers of the coca plant, from which cocaine is derived, to stop growing the plant in the Chapare region of Bolivia. The plant had been grown and used by the Bolivian people, primarily the indigenous Indian population, for medicinal purposes (holistic medicine) for centuries.

The program was called the "Coca Eradication Program." Eradicate is a strong word. Eradicate a centuries old custom, tradition and life style? Solution - Change the name of the program to the "Coca Reduction Program." You can reduce to zero, right? If you do that (and in my opinion in this case, you won't), you have eradicated the plant. But, you have done so in a way that makes it more palatable to people. You may have to apply different strokes to different folks.

Let's carry the above example one step further in the real world. As I mentioned, in my opinion you will never completely eliminate the growing of the coca plant. Why? Again, local consumption of the leaf by the indigenous populace and its potential use as a herbal medicine will not allow it. One possible solution is to try to estimate local consumption needs and legal uses of the coca leaf and its extract. This will lead to an estimate of how much of the plant should be grown.

Now we've created another set of problems that need to be addressed and resolved - How do you get all parties to agree on the number of hectares that can be used to grow the plant and in what areas they could be grown in? Strokin' and education of all parties will play a major role in making something like this acceptable to most people. I said acceptable to most people because some will undoubtedly challenge the "acceptable" level yardstick.

Some of you may have picked up on the "politically correct" theme here - the involvement of governments in shaping not only their national but private sector policy as well. Think about what James Freeman Clark said: "A politician thinks of the next election; a statesman thinks of the next generation."

As a more effective manager, think of yourself as a statesman, not as a politician. What can you do to carry on the traditions of the company/organization to the next generation of employees and to the next generation of customers?

Strokin' works, no jokin'.

Reality Check: We sometimes confuse strokin' with bullshitin'. There's a big difference between the two and a good number of more effective manager recognize this. GOOD.

A SENSE OF HUMOR:

A More Effective Manager maintains a sense of humor.

Right, what the hell does a sense of humor have to do with being a more effective manager? Good question.

All I know is that if you don't have one, those eight hours days will seem to last at least ten or twelve hours, if not longer. You'll be a candidate for the funny farm in no time at all. Lighten up big guy - on staff, on coworkers, on customers and on yourself. Put some fun into the work environment.

Appreciate the fact that humor can play a role in the way that we communicate with others. It may even help us get a point across. It definitely lowers stress in the work environment.

I had an administrative Non-commissioned officer (NCO) working with me at one time. His last name was Isobe. Sometimes he was affectionately referred to as Sergeant S.O.B. He had one glass eye.

Depending on the situation and timing, if someone came in who didn't know that he had a glass eye, I would give them something to take to Isobe with the comment to; "Ask Sergeant Isobe to keep an eye on it." If they did say that, Isobe never missed a cue. He'd reach up and pluck his glass eye out of its socket and put it on the paper. The reaction of the person led to many laughs in the office.

The company driver we had in the Army unit that I was assigned to when stationed in Germany (2/15th, 3rd Infantry Division), was an enlisted man. Believe it or not his first name was "General." His last name was Bradley. You got it. Whenever a new officer came into the Battalion, we'd give him a call and tell him that General Bradley would be down to inspect his area in the next half hour or so. These new arrivals would be jitterier than a long tailed cat in a room full of rocking chairs. The look on their faces when "General" Bradley reported to them and they saw his name-tag was; priceless.

An incident that not only displayed perseverance on the part of an employee, yet one that also tickled my funny bone involved a U.S. Government employee requesting additional lodging monies. The hotel that he was scheduled to stay in for one night cost seven dollars more than what he was authorized to spend.

After discussing this with the controller's office he was told that this additional money had to be authorized prior to his departure. The bottom line was that this professional employee wrote a one page justification and hand carried it around to obtain the clearances from several different staff officers and then presented it to the final approving authority.

A fellow coworker and I estimated that the time it took this person to compose and write the justification and obtain the clearances and final signature was in the neighborhood of two hours. The estimated cost was probably a couple of hundred dollars as he was a mid-level professional. But, how about the time of the other people who had to read and clear his justification? The two hours that this mid level professional could have used differently?

Was this humorous to me? You bet. What put a smile on my face was see-ing this guy walking down the hall in his baggy pants, tennis shoes, sun-burst colored tie and unkempt hair with a big grin on his face. In addition to the ten-thousand mile round-trip boondoggle that he was going on, that cost several thousands of dollars, he also got forty-nine more dollars out of Uncle Sugar.

Granted, you probably see fewer incidents like the one mentioned above in the private sector. The incident is still noteworthy, because it brings into play various elements that a manager and management should be aware of. This guy really believed that he should do this. He was persistent. Management really believed that this was the correct way for this to be processed; persistency, or a tunnel vision approach to procedures? Did the mean really justify the end? Was it time to change the paradigm? Was it time for some reengineering of procedures?

A more recent bit of humor was in an exchange of emails. One of my USAID colleagues, and friend was tasked to organize the Fourth of July shindig in a small European country which was hosted by the American Ambassador. As one can imagine, the event included a gaggle of foreign diplomats and host country dignitaries and officials. While this was normally done by the Management Officer at the Embassy my friend was asked to do this; no doubt because of his organizational and communication skills and, sense of humor.

Since this was something that he not done before, he sent out an email ask-ing some of his colleagues for suggestions and best practices as to how to make this the best Fourth of July event that the country had every seen. Some the responses follow.

> *"If it were Lima [Peru] I would order up lots of pisco sour and cebiche."*

> *"You're a Patriots fan – book Brady and Bruschi"*

And, from the hands down winner came these comments:

> *"Are you kidding? I work my ass off not to be at post during the 4th of July! On those occasions where I have been forced to be at post I have seen several of the following options work with some degree of success; you may want to try:*
> * *Wear red, green, black and yellow – twist your hair into locks and claim to be Jamaican.*
>
> * *Shave your head; wear an orange toga, walk around bare foot weeks before July 4th and people will think that you are a monk – w/out a clue.*
>
> * *If there's an American based hotel in town – negotiate a deal with them to use their ballroom. Set it up with flags, streamers, food tables with finger*

food throughout the room. A podium or dais for dignitaries to pontificate from. Make sure that they have sufficient staff to keep the booze flowing. No cash bar that's just plain old tacky.

- *Put up bail for Michael Jackson, get an American company to pay for transportation, legal fees, etc. and get him to perform. If not, get one of the local bands to start practicing now on playing the down home Cajun, southern California dreaming, and Appalachia folk tunes – no Dixie please.*

- *Depending on the weather in July – you may want to consider an out-side venue. If so, get the air force to fly over at the precise moment the Ambassador is reading the message from GW, with red, white and blue smoke coming from their tail wings.*

- *I hear that Colin Powel will be making the public speaking circuit since he is out of a job – book him now. He will surely draw the crowds.*

- *Alternatively, you could hide and pretend not to be an American or feign ignorance about what happened at the tea party.*

Hope this helps. Best regards."

Maintain a sense of humor. The old farmer said; "If you don't have a sense of humor, you probably don't have any sense at all."

Reality Check: Most managers don't laugh, smile or pull a shenanigan or two often enough. NOT GOOD.

QUESTIONING:
A More Effective Manager asks questions.

Who first said, "Seek and ye shall find?

I was sitting in a small airfield in some God forsaken place in Vietnam trying to get back to our base camp. I was coming back from a forward administrative support area. A C-130 transport airplane would come in a couple of times a day on unscheduled flights. The load master would load emergency cargo on first and then soldiers going home or on Rest and Recuperation (R&R). This was followed by booking senior ranking military officers and then guys like me.

I was sitting around for two days and kept getting "bumped" as more prior-ity cargo or people showed up. Finally, on a flight on the third day I ran out on the tarmac to the plane and yelled up to the pilot over the roar of the engines, "Ya got room for one more." The guy looked down at me, waved his hand at the masses waiting for the next plane and said, "Look at all those guys sittin' over there, why should I take you?" I replied, "Because I'm the one here asking you, not them."

He told me to hop aboard and away we flew. Jeeze, I probably could have spent the rest of my tour waiting for a flight.

In the work environment, a more effective manager asks questions to his supervisor, to subordinates, to co-workers and to customers. "What - ask a subordinate a question? He'll think that I'm stupid." Wrong. He will know that you have an interest in his work and that you care about what he is doing.

What? - Ask my boss a question about something? She'll think that I'm not only stupid, but that I don't know what's going on? Wrong. She will know that you want to have a clear picture of what she wants done so that the job will get completed right the first time.

How much time and money is lost because we have to redo something because we did not clearly understand what was really expected from us in the first place? Asking questions allows us to reach our goals in the most efficient way.

Whatever you do, do not be afraid to ask the question, "Why?" Why are we doing this like this? Why are we redesigning this form? Why do our customers like this? Why did she get angry? The answer to the "Why" question should lead to more efficient utilization of your human and financial resources. It may also lead to what is now vogue in some management circles; a paradigm shift, or change in the way we do business.

What are we doing in the public sector now? We are reinventing government. To me the word reinventing has strong connotations. It infers that the system, and therefore the people who make up the system are so fouled up that the only way to correct whatever it is that needs to be corrected is to start all over again. Do we really need to do that?

Why do we have to reinvent government? Why not modify existing systems and make them more efficient? Why not try to educate employees to make them more proficient and productive in what they do? Why not try to change or modify federal employee behavior and work habits to allow for more creativity and input into the existing system?

Asking questions educates you and allows you to find out what people in your work environment think and what your customers want or expect. In negotiations, asking questions helps you to find out what the other side wants. In all cases, finding answers to your questions will help you make decisions and manage more intelligently and more effectively.

Asking questions is also an avenue to enhance your situational awareness. What is situational awareness? To me it is that ability to know what's going on around you. A 360 degree assessment of whatever it is that you need to assess, or whatever it is that you have an interest in or whatever it is that you want to learn about. Keeping abreast of what is going on in your office or shop, in your company and industry is important. *It's true; an informed manager is a more effective manager.*

I will mention this concept again although everyone may not agree with it. A more effective manager should encourage subordinates and/or co-workers to challenge his decisions and thought process. One way of doing this is by encouraging others to ask questions concerning your decisions. It will undoubtedly help you to focus on the issue.

It's a legitimate statement: "There is no such thing as a stupid question."

The time tested five W's are valid: Who? What? Where? When? Why? To me they should be: Why? What? Where? When? Who?

On the flip side, a wiser manager also knows when to *stop* asking why. He doesn't let asking questions lead to procrastination or delays in the decision making process. Why did the chicken cross the road? Why do you need a reason?

Ask Questions.

Reality Check:

Most managers know when to ask "Why?" (GOOD). Unfortunately, too many of them do not know when to stop asking "Why?" NOT GOOD.

ORDER IN YOUR DISORDER:

A More Effective Manager knows that there is order in his disorder.

I was thinking about this deleting this item until a new supervisor arrived. It didn't take more that one week until you couldn't see his desk. You literally had to walk on tip-toes to avoid stepping on papers that were scattered about the floor.

Putting order in your disorder is another way of saying, "Organize yourself in your own way." I'm not referring here to organizing the work force or your ability to coordinate the various elements in the work environment. What I am referring to now is your own organization in your office or cubical.

As long as you know where things are, why worry about how your desk looks? What about the perception that if you sit behind a messy desk, you are not an organized person? So what! On the other hand, what about the perception that if you sit behind an empty desk, you have nothing to do?

There is no magic formula for organizing one's self. What's important is to organize yourself in such a way whereby you can set your own pace; a pace that will allow you to execute your work plan without putting extra pressure on yourself. Try to avoid, at all cost the stress that leads to frustration and mental anguish and physical deterioration. Think about it as time management of yourself.

Try to allow enough time in the day to handle those unexpected, last minute telephone calls or invitations to meetings or to "quality circle" sessions. Believe me it is not that difficult to do. And organizing yourself will lead to what; making good use of time.

As you may have guessed already, this element does not only include time management. It also includes something along the lines of space management and industrial engineering; the layout of your office for example.

Do you like working from left to right, or right to left? Is the telephone easy to reach? A pad and pencil nearby?

The location of my computer keyboard was always a sore point with me. In most normal office configurations, this meant that I had to shift to a work station on either side of my desk, similar to the office I occupied shown in the photo on the back cover.

My solution to this may not have been unique. I had the center drawer of my desk removed and a pullout tray installed. My screen was on the left side of my desk. I had easy access to my keyboard (it slid in and out) and the screen was located so that it could not be read by my frequent visitors. It did not obstruct my line of sight to people who came into my office to sit and chat or to discuss business or to bitch. This configuration was copied by several of my colleagues.

Some of you may have noticed that the photo on the back cover is an oxymoron to what I just mentioned in the previous paragraph. The office furniture that I inherited was not conducive to the changes that I would have liked to have made. What was my solution to this dilemma? Grin and bear it, keep a positive attitude, don't whine and make the best of it.

First things first - get yourself in order and then take it to the workplace. Now that you're comfortable with your office and on a roll, take a look at the bigger picture. Space planning not only includes moving things around within your office, but the work environment as well. Through this discussion we have added the dimension of *space management* to this puzzle.

The Branch Chief position I filled at Fort Monmouth, New Jersey had four sections located in five different, converted World War II barracks. Three sections filled the top and bottom floors of three separate buildings. The other section occupied the bottom floors of the fourth and fifth building. Why? Who knows? But, it seemed like an easy solution to me. Move one of the split groups to one of the vacant top floors.

Now the fun began. Coordination with the Post Engineer included finding solutions to plumbing, heating, insulation, roofing and electrical installation and structural issues because of the additional weight of office equipment and furniture that would be added to the second floor. All of this was doable. Three months later we moved and had a more customer friendly and better work environment.

Was there resistance by staff to this change? You better believe it.

Be organized, but do it in your own way. There is order in your disorder.

Reality Check: Most managers do a pretty good job at organizing themselves in the work environment. GOOD.

CHAPTER IV

————◆————

CLOSING

THAT'S ALL FOLKS. Managing people in the real world work environment and more effective management is not that difficult once you identify, and become fully aware of those elements that are involved in it - Those pieces that will solve/resolve any of your management puzzles.

Focus on those elements that you believe are needed to more effectively manage whomever/whatever it is that you want to manage. Put these awareness elements to work for you. Implement them. Integrate them into your daily management routine.

It is important to remember that you have flexibility in putting your management puzzle together. These awareness elements are the parts that you need to complete the puzzle.

I may have missed some areas that you feel are important. That's OK. Why? Because I started you thinking along the lines of being "aware" of what more effective management involves; different factors. Add to this list whatever it is that you think is missing. Write down the reasons why you think it is (they are) important.

You may think that some of the elements that I have mentioned here do not apply to you. No problem...no problema...mafishe moshkela...pas de problem... Nyet problema - Trash 'em.

Continually evaluate your performance as a manager and the performance of the people who surround you. *Develop a positive attitude* and *become a "people oriented" person.* Don't forget that, "You get what you give." You don't have to be arrogant to be successful or effective. Throw in a little bit of luck and use some common sense.

Reread this book every once in a while and listen to what is being said between its covers. You are on your way to becoming a better and more effective manager in the real fast-paced, multi-dimensional work environment. It's not that difficult. Good luck... Dave.

i

AUTHOR'S AFTERWORD

I SKETCHED THE first outline of this book while in La Paz, Bolivia, a while ago. Patience is one of my virtues.

While in Bolivia I decided to change job location and I applied for, and was selected for the position of the Supervisory General Services Officer with the United States Agency for International Development (USAID), Cairo, Egypt. This was, and still may be the largest USAID Mission in the world. It was also superbly managed, the "benchmark" Mission in the Eastern hemisphere, if not in the world. Accepting this position meant bigger challenges, and potentially, bigger headaches as well. No pain, no gain right?

On the positive side, I was reunited with my ex-boss from the USAID Mission in La Paz, Bolivia and I looked forward to complementing the successful management team that he headed in Cairo. It also gave my wife the opportunity to semi-retire and re-kindle her love of painting. I packed one suitcase and was off to Cairo on 22 September 1993.

During my stay in Cairo I also completed and obtained a Masters' degree in Business Management from LaSalle University. My thesis was: The Identification and Analysis of Business Risks in an Overseas Environment: the Bolivian Experience which I researched and wrote in the mid 1980's. It is interesting to note that, in my opinion my findings presented in this thesis are just as valid today as they were in the mid-80s.

USAID Cairo was followed by a truncated tour in Almaty, Kazakhstan that lasted some twenty months, four months between jobs, more than five years in Kiev, Ukraine and a tour in Montenegro.

While in Cairo, myself along with some of my colleagues went through a perplexing period of watching Washington politicians try to micromanage well-managed government Agency's, like the USAID. They advocated the creation of a new age, super Department of State by merging other agencies into it. The momentum got stronger in the next years. Is it time to stop the insanity? Let me rock the boat little now.

There may be different thoughts and ideas on ways to arrive at a New World Order or how to make the world a better place to live in. My thoughts center

ii

around three major areas: 1. *Diplomacy and political influence,* by any government on another government to bring about peaceful change in governance and rule of law; 2. *Economic growth and sustainability* that may be attained by debt restructure, currency/interest manipulation, trade restrictions, redistribution of wealth or whatever, and, 3. *Humanitarian/economic assistance* primarily at grass roots level in areas such as improving infrastructures, health services, education and the environment and the creation or stimulation of job markets. There is a fourth; through military options including assistance or intervention.

An emphasis, starting around 2004 I believe in Washington was to focus on the three D's; Diplomacy, Development and Defense. I can buy into that. This tri-pod approach allows for adjustments to any of the legs (primarily caused by intra-agency squabbles over funding) and still lends itself to maintaining a stable platform that they support; i.e. making the world a better place to live in. What I cannot buy into is the merging of the USAID into the Department of State.

Merging the United States Agency for International Development into the Department of State makes no sense. One agency holding two of the three "D" cards; Diplomacy and Development gives too much power and control to that entity. My gut feeling tells me that what will come out of this is: "If you don't do it my way (through Diplomacy) we'll reduce Development funding/ programs." One entity holding both the carrot and the stick could proliferate, rather than reduce the image of "Yankee" imposed capitalism/imperialism.

Plus, the creation of a humongous organization will lead to even greater inefficiencies that exist within each organization now. This will not streamline processes but only create more bureaucracy and bottlenecks. You will wind up with "reverse synergism."

The State Department's primary business is Diplomacy; USAID's primary business is Development. In my opinion proponents of merging USAID into the DOS are trying to mix oil and water and, have their heads where the sun doesn't shine; i.e. in the sand next to the ostrich.

Let's take that "half step to the rear" for a minute. The following was pulled from the internet and is reprinted verbatim.

> *"On September 4, 1961, the Congress passed the Foreign Assistance Act which reorganized the U.S. foreign assistance programs including separating military and non-military aid. The Act mandated the creation of an agency to administer economic assistance programs. On November 3, 1961 President John F. Kennedy established the U.S. Agency for International Development (USAID).*
> *USAID became the first U.S. foreign assistance organization whose primary emphasis was on long-range economic and social development assistance efforts.*
> ***Freed from political and military functions*** *[my emphasis] that plagued its predecessor organizations, USAID was able to offer direct support to the develop-*

ing nations of the world.

The agency unified already existing U.S. foreign aid efforts, combining the economic and technical assistance operations of the International Cooperation Agency, the loan activities of the Development Loan Fund, the local currency functions of the Export-Import Bank, and the agricultural surplus distribution activities of the Food for Peace program of the Department of Agriculture."

The merger of the United States Information Agency (USIA) and the United States Arms Control and Disarmament Agency (ACDA) into the Department of State in the late 1990's early 2000's made more sense. The ACDA was an independent agency for thirty-eight years until it was gobbled up by the DOS. It served its' purpose under both Republican and Democratic administrations. Its' role, while vital involved only the highest level of government officials in negotiations that led to treaties such as the Strategic Arms Limitation Talks (SALT).

The USIA served as the mouthpiece and propaganda machine for the USG in its battle against the evil communist empire headed by the USSR. Since the break up of the Soviet Union this agency's role is more in line with defining the political will of the United States to bring change to foreign government thinking through what is now labeled transformational diplomacy.

Humanitarian and economic assistance directly involves the heart and soul of any nation – its' people. The design and planning and implementation of this assistance must be kept under separate cover.

Douglas Casey, a classmate of Bill Clinton at Georgetown University reportedly said that: "Foreign aid might be defined as a transfer of money from poor people in rich countries to rich people in poor countries." There might be some truth to this. That is all the more reason for a USAID type, hands-on approach to humanitarian assistance programs.

Humanitarian assistance programs are not failing because the rich get richer. They are failing because governments have lost focus on grass-roots programs. These cannot be replaced by donations and give-a-ways.

The replacement of a political ism should strengthen humanitarian efforts amongst donor countries while not deepening the crevasse between them. Recipients and donors must be active participants and shareholders in the process.

It would make more sense to me to consider merging the Peace Corps (PC) with USAID. Both have the same basic goals and objectives – to make the world a better place to live in – through humanitarian assistance programs.

USAID is in a better position to hammer on the concept of trading bullets for butter. The Department of State is in a better position of hammering on political heads.

The continued separation of these two entities should still create a framework within the government that will allow those in the Executive and Legislative

Branch to view these areas more objectively. The further consolidation of these will only lead to more centralization and, even more frightening, more power, control and influence within a restricted, tight group of people in the most powerful and already overly bureaucratic nation in the world.

Rather than roll USAID into the Department of State, I would play the devil's advocate and recommend a rather brash approach. Like the creation of the Department of Homeland Security, someone should consider creating a new cabinet post – Department of Domestic and International Humanitarian Aid.

Humanitarian assistance (Development) should be a full partner with Diplomacy and Defense in bringing about a new world order. This concept not only dictates, but demands a separate cabinet post.

Let's not wait for any other major catastrophe to happen to open our eyes. I recently heard that 800 million people are at starvation levels. Hello. An agency like the USAID *must*, not should, but *must* take the lead in the area of using humanitarian measures to bring about world peace and harmony.

Before even more people, within our own country or in foreign countries become undernourished or slip to poverty levels of subsistence, let's be proactive and look at ways to better utilize food surpluses; use our military reserve units to build roads and clinics and install Bailey bridges and water purification plants; improve literacy rates and educate people about sexually transmitted diseases, the environment and whatnot and administer rural shot and mobile clinic programs.

Before looking for ways to create gigantic agencies that will undoubtedly become only more bureaucratic and less efficient, Uncle Sam should be looking at further ways to make existing agencies more efficient. Spinning-off parts of inefficient operations should be looked at more closely. This spin off may mean looking for private sector entities to perform the same or similar services or functions now being performed by a government agency. But, even if that happens, what checks and balances are in place to see that Uncle Sugar doesn't get ripped off by his own people, let alone foreign graft and corruption.

Let me stop my own rambling here, lest I go on to suggest the abolishment of the United States Marine Corps. Their ground forces integrated into the Army and their fixed wing air support units into the Air Force. This, in my opinion is just as far fetched as creating a super Department of State (or any other super department for that matter).

I was also pleased to read that Congress is or will consider the term limit issue. They are considering legislation that would limit both House and Senate members to twelve consecutive years in office. I believe that this is too short a period for these elected officials. I would personally like to see this read along the lines of eighteen or twenty consecutive years, or a total thereof, which ever comes first.

Government employees, just like their private-sector counterparts should be trained and encouraged to become more efficient and more effective, to be creative and to take risks.

On the management side, more effective managers equate to better companies, and governments.

AUTHOR'S BIOGRAPHY

MR. KORPONAI HAS been with the United States Agency for International Development since January 1991. He served in Bolivia as the Supervisory General Service's Officer and Deputy Executive Officer, in Egypt as the Supervisory General Service's Officer, in Kazakhstan as the Executive Officer, in the Ukraine as the Deputy Executive Officer and in Montenegro as the Executive Officer.

These management and logistical support activities provided services to over hundreds of American employees and their families and Foreign Service National employees.

He also played key roles in developing Mission procurement plans and operating expense budgets; developing, drafting and implementing internal Mission management systems and policies; conducting management assessments; contract negotiations; developing and writing Statements of Work; and, coordinating security issues with USAID and American embassy personnel.

Prior to working with USAID, he worked for two large American companies in Bolivia. He was the administrative/financial manager for a 68 million U.S. dollar road construction project being built between La Paz and Cotapata Bolivia by the S.J. Groves & Sons Company, Minneapolis, Minnesota.

After S.J. Groves he was the South American representative for the R. A. Hanson Company, Spokane, Washington. This company was involved in mining activities and the manufacture of mining and specialty equipment. In addition to his work in Bolivia he traveled to Chile, Ecuador and Brazil and assessed mining potentials. In Chile he also established a network that led to the sale of equipment there.

Mr. Korponai was honorably discharged from the United States Army in 1978 at the rank of Captain. His overseas tours included Germany, Vietnam (two tours) and Bolivia. He was retired from the United States Army Reserves at the rank of Major.

He graduated from the University of Connecticut in 1964 with a B.S. in Physical Education and from LaSalle University in 1994 with a Master's degree in Business Management.

He is married and has three grown children and five grandchildren.